The Emperor

Psychology

by

Steven Saunders

 HOLIGRAL

First Edition, 2011 AD

© Steven Saunders 2011

Published by The Holigral Partnership
7 Three Hill View, Glastonbury, Somerset BA6 8AU, England
holigral.com

British Library Cataloguing in Publication Data
Saunders, Steven, 1960-
The Emperor's New Psychology

ISBN 978-0-9570409-0-8

HOLIGRAL

CONTENTS

Cover illustration by Nicholas Drew.

1 Introduction

"If Alice is to enter Wonderland, then she had better follow the white rabbit, and be sure to come back out again."

1.1 Blundering in the Beginning

When the first European explorers entered the Amazonian lands they had no maps, and legends abounded as to fantastical and mythical treasures and peoples. Gradually the world has been mapped, the mystique perhaps lost, but anyone can now travel freely and with confidence. Understanding the human mind has been the same, realistically. But now there is a complete map, enabling safe and complete journeys into and through the formerly unknown territories.

If only one person has this map they are rightly considered the emperor. If we all have the map, then no-one need get lost, and indeed, everyone can find their way out, and into the light, where they will see that all the emperors are indeed naked.

The Holigral Method is a complete set of models and processes designed to sort out one's life, to make sense of the world around, and indeed to then prosper and enjoy life to the full. The processes enable people to undo faulty maps and move in the daylight, where all can be seen and understood. This is done by using patterns of questions based upon the underlying models of how minds are structured; upon the skeleton keys to all of Pandora's boxes, hidden among the far recesses, nooks and crannies of the deep unconscious. After enough journeys one can trust the skeleton keys, and then learn to use them for all circumstances.

This book covers the models, processes, transcripts, consequences and analysis, and also, the story of how I made a map that is indeed isomorphic to how the mind and selves are structured. Like anyone stumbling around in the dark, who eventually finds their way out, there were many lucky accidents, and no little help from others also wandering around, with more or less purpose. And now, if you are sitting comfortably, then I will begin.

In the beginning, once upon a time, in a land far, far away ...

My paternal grandfather was a "traveller"; a fairground strongman from Ireland, who ended up with his own business involving casting, lead works and structural steelwork. He played cricket for Surrey 2nd XI, football for Crystal Palace, was capable of columns of mental seven-figure arithmetic, mirror writing, master-quality metalworking and woodworking; a polymath and a mystic initiate.

He was literally a "renaissance man" of the early 20th Century. Living in those giant footsteps, was my father, a metallurgist-engineer, with a noisy factory full of welding sparks, smelting vapours and grinding sounds. He committed suicide in 1992, an event which contributed to my interest in psychology. What makes a person reach that point of despair or hopelessness? What can anyone [else] do about it? And how do those affected by events like suicide deal with their feelings and the rest of the family?

In reaction to the factory's assault on my senses, I chose to go into applied mathematics and physics, which was much more peaceful and quiet. For over twenty years, I researched and developed systems in engineering companies; on radars, signals intelligence[1] and the like, employing signal

---

[1] Signals intelligence involves the gathering of electronic signals from environments in order to understand a situation, such as a battlefield or a war zone, to then be able to assess the situation, make assessments of threats and then take appropriate minimum risk actions.

Whether we realise it or not, humans do this naturally, mostly as a background unconscious activity. Even walking down the road, or visiting a new bar will involve some level of scanning and threat assessment. The technology reflects the minds that made it, and therefore the methods and systems seem to be appropriate for understanding some aspects of human activity.

8

processing[2], neural networks[3] and pattern recognition techniques[4] in the creative process. But, I never called myself an engineer; not until after I had left the industry - even though I was chartered.

My maternal grandmother seemed to me to be the embodiment of calm and acceptance; she had grace and presence, and had all the time in the world for a host of grandchildren. My mother, named after her mother, was conceived, carried and born during the Blitz of 1940. After raising me and my siblings, she became a psychotherapist and a social worker, seeking out and working with, what seemed to me at the time, most outlandish folk, like the Sufi Master[5] Frank (Faisal) Khan, grandson of "The Prophet", Inayat Khan - and others even more "out there" from my world view of the time.

So perhaps inevitably, having grown my own team of research engineers, I became ever more interested in people and how they worked, rather than in the machines and computers we were developing, that merely emulated people. Books and courses introduced me to the subject, and gradually I took on my own experimenting. After a few years of doing this part-time, in 2004 I gave up my engineering life and focussed all my efforts in this direction.

---

[2] Signal processing is the branch of technology associated with measuring, conditioning, transforming and identifying electronic signals. It is the underpinning technology of signals intelligence, radar and radio.

[3] Neural networks are simplified technical models designed to emulate how the brain works, and to therefore use the models for tasks such as matching or identifying measured objects with a library of previously measured objects.

[4] Pattern recognition is the branch of mathematics associated literally with recognising and matching patterns of data. It is used for DNA matching in forensic laboratories, number plate recognition for automated speed traps, and aircraft identification, among a myriad of other modern applications.

[5] A Sufi is a member of a particular Islamic group who accept an underlying truth in all beliefs and religions. They are often characterised by their whirling-dancing, and advocate living a life without judgement, beyond right and wrong, as exemplified by the poet Rumi, the prophet Inayat Khan and the wise fool, Nasruddin.

I found that every single influence in my life was necessary and contributing towards my understanding of human nature, and I set about consciously applying Physics to the problems of humans today, very much with the hindsight of applying principles to what I had experientially learned. In other words, I fitted the theory to the empirical information, not the other way around. This, I will show, as the book progresses; fitting models-to-observations, not world-to-model.

In "The Lord of the Rings", the character Tom Bombadil tells the four Hobbits the truths and stories about the deep, dark secrets of the world, normally hidden from everyday folk. Much of this was uncomfortable to hear. I apologise now, but really, if I am to present the entire structure of reality and the consequences, the reader had better be ready for a descent into the Underworld and beyond. And with no more ado, let us be on our way.

1.2 A Physicist's Perspective

"Everything should be made as simple as possible but not one bit simpler." Albert Einstein

A good physicist will observe first and then seek a hypothesis that can explain that which has been observed; they theorise in hindsight. If the hypothesis predicts phenomena which are also observed, then even better, it can become a "theory". Hindsight rules.

There are scientists who theorise first and then look to see whether the world fits the theory, but this approach is more prone to unconsciously ignoring the data that does not fit the theory. As time goes by the ego can attach to the theory and the scientist becomes blind to the data that disproves the theory.

I personally believe that every theory has a blind spot and that we need mutually contradictory theories, we need paradox to more fully explain nature, and that any theory has its limits, due to its assumptions. However, what if there were a theory that could explain all?

As this is my personal sense of a physicist's perspective on human nature, the journey is through observation first and theory later. This is followed by making predictions, so that the theory can be tested.

I require a theory that makes both creationists and darwinians right, a theory that includes the metaphysical and the physical; a theory that can include both ghosts able to be existing and also to be only figments of the imagination of the perceiver.

"...when you have eliminated the impossible, whatever remains, however improbable, must be the truth.", Sherlock Holmes in "The Sign of the Four", Sir Arthur Conan Doyle.

Why do we behave the way we do? Why do we say the things that we say, and hold the beliefs that we have? What would have had to have been true, in order for a person to have become the way that they are now? And what can be observed and thus deduced about this? These are some of the questions sponsoring the thought experiments, the observations, deductions and analyses presented.

Understanding how and why people become the way they are is a science, a study of the highest complexity. I spent over twenty years in cutting-edge engineering research and development, making systems that sought, in limited ways, to emulate human beings. I did not realise at the time, but the technical research, the very engineering development processes used, and the enquiring mind honed in those years, were uniquely combined to create an ability to innovate and invent almost anything.

The biggest challenges were to understand and heal human beings, and beyond that, to understand and heal groups and cultures. This represents my life's work.

"The significant problems we have cannot be solved at the same level of thinking with which we created them." Albert Einstein.

We live in times that demand ever-more narrow niches and areas of expertise, whether it is by forces of market discrimination or from the variety and complexity of modern life. In such times a person can be so focussed on their niche that they miss the domain, because of the over-training of their brain's neural network in their specialised niche.

For example, when training a computer simulation of a neural network, its performance relates to how it has been trained[6].

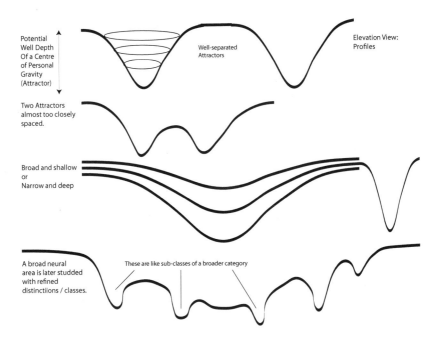

Potential Well Depth Of a Centre of Personal Gravity (Attractor)

Well-separated Attractors

Elevation View: Profiles

Two Attractors almost too closely spaced.

Broad and shallow or Narrow and deep

A broad neural area is later studded with refined distinctiions / classes.

These are like sub-classes of a broader category

Profile view of classes set within classes

[6] The training of Neural Networks is briefly described in wikipedia, but "Bishop, C.M. (1995) Neural Networks for Pattern Recognition, Oxford University Press. ISBN 0-19-853849-9" is an excellent text for more in-depth study.

If broad classifying ranges[7] are developed first, and refined discriminations[8] are added later, without too much training data, the network has an ability to generalise and address the boundaries between classes smoothly.

If the network is over-trained then the classes it recognises become too specific and much data cannot be reliably classified - the boundaries become inflexible and blind spots develop. As this is a computer simulation being modelled on the human exemplar, it is reasonable to infer that over-niching is making humans less flexible and even potentially less flexible within their own domain of interest.

A person coming into a new field, without prior teaching of the "known expertise" will often have just this more general neural connectivity - they will appear less niche-expert for sure, but they may see that which is in the expert's blind spot, or ask the perfect awkward question that leads to something new. And physicists do ask the awkward question "why?"

Michael Faraday is an example of the untrained incomer joining the world of physics and chemistry[9]. He served a seven year apprenticeship as a bookbinder and bookseller, and consequently had the expected hard time gaining recognition as a genuine scientist; he refused many honours in return. His contribution advanced both Physics and Chemistry greatly.

The hero of Isaac Asimov's "Foundation" series, Hari Seldon, had an untrained natural, Yugo Amaryl, as his second in command throughout the development of "Psychohistory"[10].

Einstein kept a picture of Faraday on his wall, together with pictures of Newton and Maxwell. David Grove, with whom I collaborated in 2005-6, wanted to gather the pictures of the eminent scientists whose theories we

---

[7] A classifying range in a self-organising neural network is the spread that a class or a set of classes covers. A broad range means that, later, it has the capacity to develop sub-classes and to smoothly manage the boundaries between classes. A narrow range is likely to prove unstable in the longer term.

[8] Discrimination is the term used in pattern recognition for the ability to decide to which class a measurement belongs. It is a kind of decision making.

[9] See his biography on wikipedia, and also the bios there for Newton, Einstein and company.

[10] Isaac Asimov's Foundation Series of novels.

were using to explain the work. Like Einstein, he gathered inspiration from the faces of these people.

As Faraday himself found, exchanging views with fellow professionals from other disciplines can lead to a flood of new insights for all involved. He toured Europe, assisting Humphrey Davy, meeting the top experts in Physics and Chemistry, and then followed this up with a string of inventions.

The Biophysicist might know less in Physics or Biology than the experts focussed on one area, but his different neural connectivity may give rise to a broader capacity to generalise rules and develop new science. A child raised bilingually takes longer initially to learn the languages but later in life their ability to acquire new learning is well known to be greater, as is their ability to grasp new concepts faster[11].

Consider the native american quote "white man speaks with forked tongue." In the anglo-saxon world this is interpreted as saying that "white man lies" - due to the mythological root of the serpent in Genesis. But the native American has no such mythology. Instead he has a language that implicitly combines both object and moving, both relational and flow, as seen in their names: "Crazy Horse, "Sitting Bull", "Running Bear".

What he is actually trying to communicate, is a concept that is difficult to express in English, because it is a blind spot of the English language. This is, approximately: "The very language you are speaking, the way you are speaking, and the energy we are feeling means that separating is happening between you, the speaker, from us, the spoken-to, and therefore we are not feeling trusting, because communicating is not happening 'as one whole experience'."

Only having one language in which to speak and think constrains the whole system. Ideas can be thought in one language but not in the other, but having both languages gives the person greater flexibility of thought and insight.

Probably the greatest genius of all time, Leonardo da Vinci, was a polymath, a person who was able to turn his considerable intellect to many different disciplines. An expert in art, he made great contributions to science, engineering and manufacturing, both famous and unsung.

---

[11] See "http://www.eurekalert.org/pub_releases/2003-11/sfn-ssb111103.php" as one example of a reference study.

"In physics, your solution should convince a reasonable person. In math, you have to convince a person who's trying to make trouble. Ultimately, in physics, you're hoping to convince Nature. And I've found Nature to be pretty reasonable."
Frank Wilczek

Natural Philosophy

"It should be possible to explain the laws of physics to a barmaid." Albert Einstein

The modern world of physics is the study of the physical world, about forces of nature: thermodynamics, gases and pressure, the laws of motion, gravity, fluid mechanics, optics and electromagnetism, relativity and quantum; and for some, the search for a unified theory. Or in the pub explanation, it is about understanding how things work and using that understanding to invent new stuff.

Natural Philosophy is what Physics was called in Newton's day[12]. Physics was not then exclusively physical, but also included the metaphysical; the imaginary, non-physically observable. In fact none of the laws of physics can be observed, but their effects can be; the laws of physics are simply our best model that fits the experimental observations. They are not true, just good approximations.

As God and things metaphysical were increasingly separated from the *observable* natural world, "Natural Sciences" came to refer to the physically observable and "Philosophy" referred to the metaphysical, imaginary side of life. During this period of separation of religion from science, the province of God was ceded to theology and philosophy, and the province of the physical world was ceded to the sciences. Definitely a divorce of convenience at the time, does this divorce still serve our understanding of the nature of the universe in which we live?

Funnily enough, at just about the same time, De Moivre invented complex numbers to represent the imaginary mathematically. This could be a curious

---

[12] Until the 1840's what we now call science was called "natural philosophy," so that even Isaac Newton's great book on motion and gravity, published in 1687, was "The Mathematical Principles of Natural Philosophy" (*Principia Mathematica Philosophiae Naturalis*).

compensation mechanism to have something in place to cover for the loss of the "real" imaginary, could it not?

After a few hundred years, the study of Physics is returning full circle, and the observer is being re-included into the experiment[13]. Physics itself has lived a lifecycle, just like human beings do. And because the science of Physics was birthed in the minds of men, it also reveals the working of those minds; in the mirror of the science we can look and learn.

From Physics we have inventions like radar. Modern radars behave like people. For example, a radar under severe threat scans narrow sectors rapidly, wanting to get as early a glimpse of a threat as possible - just like a human will rapidly scan a group of people to assess the threat. The safer the radar's environment, the less frequent the scanning; the safer the human's environment, the more a person relaxes.

This is not surprising - radars are designed by human minds solving problems that those humans' ancestors have faced for thousands of years. The military mind has the same underlying planning process as a hunter-gathering tribe when going into the territory of a rival tribe; just like a pride of lions going out of their normal range. The science and the engineering both follow nature and reflect nature. By noticing how people scan their eyes, an observer can assess the level of threat assessment happening.

As well as being a mirror, Physics can be used as a lens to take a perspective on human development. For example, the Theory of Relativity states that there is no absolute frame of reference. Thus, there is no absolute truth, meaning that all perspectives are equally valid and that each perspective's frame of reference defines its relative observation. Relativity equates to the concept that people have different perspectives, and that none of those perspectives is absolutely right; they are relatively right. So, leading thinkers often look outside of their domain of interest to get a sufficiently different perspective on their work.

If nothing else, at least Physics serves as a useful set of metaphors for understanding what might be happening in a given situation.

---

[13] Heisenberg's Uncertainty Principle.

1.3 Systems Thinking

Adjacent to the world of engineering, and yet part of the world of understanding humans in groups, is Systems Thinking[14], which is a natural stepping stone for an engineer to take towards the world of "soft sciences". Systems Thinking is a discipline normally used for diagnosing problem patterns and cycles in business, organisations and even marketplaces, and then making structural changes to effect the required flow. It also applies to the individual human being and relationship dynamics.

The models come from analogue electronics, addressing feedback as a control or as an accelerator/decelerator. It is all about links and loops. By way of example, the following pattern shows the effect of short-term fixes.

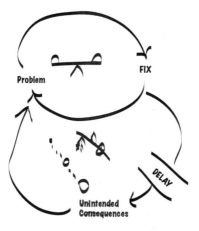

A short-term solution is used to fix a problem and it works initially. However, the fix is really only treating the symptom not the root cause. As the symptomatic fix is used more and more, so fundamental long-term corrective measures are used less. Eventually the ability to make fundamental corrections may be lost, leaving a dangerous dependence on the symptomatic solution.

The solution is to focus your attention on fundamental solutions, not symptomatic fixes. If you have to use a fix, because the fundamental solution cannot be applied yet, use it to buy time to work on the fundamental solution.

---

[14] See Peter Senge's book, "The Fifth Discipline".

In relation to the development of Holigral, the entire journey has been one of finding a fundamental model of reality that enables one to guarantee that the fundamental causes can be addressed. I moved on from model and process to model and process until I found the answers that work for me.

Systems Thinking is facilitated by asking patterns of "why is something happening?" to elicit the cycles, causes and roots in action. As it was designed for group work, no blame was allowed, and so answers going to people or inside them were banned. I broke this rule, and by using the methods shown later, there are better solutions than those possible where individual contributions are not allowed to be included. Holism requires one to look inside as well as beyond.

There are twelve archetypal patterns defined by Senge in the "Fifth Discipline", but in practice many more are possible and the actual system has to be modelled, not just matching apparent present situations to the archetypes. The key pattern of relevance to the world of psychology is the one shown above: "Fixes That Fail".

What is obvious is that the coaching and consulting trades are booming and skills are disappearing, if not already disappeared, in much of mainstream management. The more coaching there is, the less the managers will learn for themselves, the less useful mistakes get made. The nanny state grows.

However, the growth of coaching is a symptom of the nanny state, which is a consequence of the spoon-feeding education system now in place. Having two home-educated children, my family has discovered some of the horrible realities of the education system. Each subject has its way of thinking, and perfectly valid answers are not allowed by the strict marking schemes made up by the examiners, who are also part of the niche subject way of thinking[15]. After discovering this, we had to adapt by having our children learn the correct ways of answering questions in each subject. Intelligence is not taught, but jumping through hoops is.

For example, in a past IGCSE Geography paper, there was a question about flooding on the Mississippi river, the second part of which asked, "explain why rivers like the Mississippi change their course over time" (five marks). Instead of "any reasonable answer", the only acceptable answer, according to the mark scheme, was "meander migration" and explanations of this,

---

[15] Often called a meme, a thought form is a cultural belief or shared way of thinking or believing or seeing the world.

whereas there are many other valid reasons, like floods demolishing or recreating channels, and the effects of "man's intervention". This was an odd "expected" answer, given the context of flooding.

Well-trained doggies do not make for effective managers, though, as all they can see is how to jump through hoops, not what's around them. And so they need coaching to jump different hoops, or heaven-forbid, to actually see the hoop and question its existence.

1.4 Pre-History

In 1978 I decided that I wanted to do research as my life's work; I was seventeen. I took a year to work in a Government Laboratory in communications, learning practical electronics, computer programming and aspects of signal processing, before then taking my degree in mathematics and physics at Bristol University.

By October 2000 I had been working in systems engineering research and development for twenty-one years, mainly focussed on signal processing applied to understanding environments using automated pattern recognition systems and neural networks. I felt I had completed my purpose in the field of radar and electronic intelligence. I had thoroughly researched and reinvented every aspect of the technology - as far as I was concerned - and I had a technology development roadmap through to 2020, which has been still on the course predicted. I wanted another challenge.

I chose to take an NLP training, with the intention of improving my leadership skills. I do not know if it did that, but it did change my life direction. By the evening of the first day's introduction I had invented my first new NLP process[16], and a whole new world of magic was opened.

This became a journey of discovery, sharing a series of revelations and insights into human nature, ultimately leading to my unified theory of how people are as they are. I had to go far and wide beyond the confines of the NLP world, into things esoteric, magical, mystical, and full circle back to landing on the solid ground of my engineering and scientific heritage.

The result was this natural philosophy for living life and a set of methods for enabling us to transcend, transform and function well in this crazy world we call Planet Earth. This is a journey into understanding and seeing through the clothes of our own egos, through the existing psychological models that seek to explain our nature, and through the clothing of the wolves posing as shepherds in our present society.

The journey began in a research laboratory, where an engineer was trying to make computers perform complex tasks as well as humans, if not better. The engineer was me, and the time was October in the year 2000. Though I did not know it at the time, I was "quite" dissociated from my emotions; a stereotypical scientist.

The word "quite" is, of course, a euphemism for "seriously, unimaginably not connected or aware of the vast majority of emotional signals communicated between human beings, animals and even plants". I had

---

[16] Travelling home on a train that evening, I felt upset by a crying baby, and I thought, "I'm not having this". I pushed out the feeling, using a gesture of both my hands, like pushing a person away. Immediate relief. I asked about it the next day, expecting there to be a named NLP process that did this, and the trainer just shrugged, so I called it "the whoosh".

been given labels by the management tools of the day: ENTJ[17], Plant[18], Shaper, Driver/Influencer (DISC[19]), as have most people in business.

I had been developing a technology and team on the cutting edge of electronic intelligence, but not as successful as my ambition had desired. We had been growing forty percent per annum for eight straight years, we were world leaders in our specific niche, acknowledged within our corresponding UK's Governmental research circles, and with a clear map into the future. However, year on year I had the same feedback from senior managers; something about "smoothing off the rough edges". Why did I not ask "what rough edges?", why did I not say that I had absolutely no idea what these people were talking about? Clearly, I was missing something.

I just was myself, I accepted other people were as they were, and I got on with my job, developing my team, my technology and delivering my projects on time and budget. I had no idea that some other people did NOT accept people as they are, that they were constantly judging and politically analysing, that they were living in a world of unconscious fears and conditioning that seemed to have passed me by. I had no idea that other managers were receiving share options and taking the credit for my work.

I was seriously unaware of what I now call "the social matrix"[20], its power and influence, and the consequences of not living according to its code. I was just sufficiently aware, though, to recognise that I was missing something.

---

[17] ENTJ = Extroverted (not Introverted) iNtuitive (not sensing), Thinking (not Feeling), Judging (not Perceiving); part of the Myers-Briggs personality Type Indicator. Personally I disagreed completely, I felt I did all the aspects of which they spoke, and that this test, and all others like it, were flawed.

[18] A Belbin plant is an ideas person.

[19] DISC profiling is another toolkit, also, I believe, mischaracterising people and sticking them in boxes which do not really cover the range of behaviours a single person has. In hindsight, I can say that my "shape-shifting" and osmotic abilities meant that I did indeed not fit any of the boxes belonging to the left-brained world that needs to box people. If they had boxes called "tortoise" and "hare", then I'd be the hare and the tortoise, depending upon the situational needs.

[20] Matrix: by this term here, I refer to the collective, or group, unconscious.

The first psychology that I came across was actually Transactional Analysis, in the early 90's. I read the books[21], I was curious, and the models made some kind of sense; people having parent, adult and child ways of being, and the associated dynamics that go with such interactions.

Also, I could recognise the idea of games and scripts in the patterns of people around. Years later, meeting my first of many Red Riding Hoods, I was blown away by the accuracy and the simplicity of recognising the patterns and universal stories that people play out.

Following that NLP training in 2000, I spent the next ten years learning, studying, researching, developing and collaborating in the field of personal development, before finally settling upon a model and method that works, independent of language, culture, belief systems, race or religion.

1.5 Association and Dis-association

"A Whole in One."

One of the NLP processes that I learned was about discovering my values and arranging them into a hierarchy without conflict, to make for an easier life. To start, I had to identity the three most significant events in my life. This is a pretty impossible task, so I chose the three most recent significant events.

The first was an experience in the Indian Ocean. I had had a fear of sharks for as long as I could remember, and there I was, snorkelling on my own, a few hundred yards from a boat on a reef in the middle of nowhere, heart pumping, fear radiating. I had just passed a moray eel - a fearful enough creature - when I saw a white-tipped shark heading directly my way. Instantly I knew there was no running, no escape.

So I stopped and then drifted into a vertical posture, while an incredible relaxation descended through my body, like a higher power had taken over. I calmed, my heart rate dropped, and I felt no fear - none whatsoever; gone.

---

21 "Eric Berne, "The Games People Play", "What Do People Say After They Say 'Hello'?"

[Many years later a German psychiatrist told me this was "just a chemical reaction accepting death". Right!]

The shark stopped, and for what seemed like an eternity, we just gazed eye-to-eye. The eyes of a shark are death, the Grim Reaper lurks therein, and to me it felt like he said, "it's not your time." The shark turned and swam in another direction. I promptly returned to the boat; there was no point tempting fate!

This experience overlaid an earlier cycle accident, whereby in all rights I should have either died or been seriously injured. With a small slice of time missing from my memory (after the event), I went from being on the bike to sliding backwards downhill, shredding all my clothing but ending up with only a few minor cuts and bruises.

This made sense in another NLP exercise on timelines, where I had decided to "go off the end" - before conception and after death; both leading to experiences of joy and peace. Thereafter, how could I fear death? When my time is up, it's up. Until then, live!

The second experience was the birth of my daughter (who was, incidentally, one year old on the day I met the shark), a time of great joy and yet anxiety, waiting.

The third experience was a presentation at work, where after several years of effort I had finally brought the industry and all three governmental research establishments together to agree a common strategy in the field of signal processing in electronic intelligence. Getting air, sea and land combined and agreed was a vindication of my life's work at the time.

This event overlaid my father's suicide in 1992, after which I vowed never to end up like that, actually powering me into fulfilling success and destiny.

The important things around these events were written into one-word statements and then combined and ordered. However, I broke that mould. Only one thing mattered to me: to be "one". I had no idea what this meant, but my eyes were streaming with tears. So, that evening, in the Baker Street Pizza Express, my friend and co-student Chris offered to take me through an integration process.

We had already done a single parts integration process[22] beforehand, so this was, by extension, the same, just bigger. Placing my right hand on my left upper forearm, I gradually moved this hand to join the left one, integrating "all my parts" together. At least, that was the plan.

I experienced passing through two fathomless, dark, cold abysses before finding a warmth and joy I had never known. What happened next was bizarre for me. Beforehand, Chris likened me to a brazier; dark with strong beams of light shining out. Afterwards, I was the full radiant light.

"Feelings." Morris Albert

I had a surreal, some would call delusional, experience for several hours, and altered consciousness for weeks. Things happened like my mobile phone ringing on vibrate in my pocket, only for me to get it out and find it switched off; astral travelling to see Joao de Deus in Brazil and check in how he did his healing; and spinning protections for my children.

For the first time in my conscious memory I could feel the everyday feelings, feel the world like I had no recall of ever doing before. I could feel my sister's love for her newborn baby, I could feel a pregnant secretary walking along the corridor and know she was radiating serenity (while I was in an office). I could feel the world and know I was part of it.

I also knew how Jesus did his miracles, how to astral travel and many other so-called psychic skills. Beforehand, all I knew was the experience of excesses, with none of the subtleties of refined emotional discrimination.

All this faded, I now know due to the re-imposition of my structures and attractors[23]. It had been a temporary reprieve. Gradually, I developed it back into an everyday experience, but the yards were hard and there was no help.

---

[22] Parts Integration Process: in NLP there is a process called a "Visual Squash", whereby one places two "parts" of the self into each hand, and eventually one squashes them together, literally; a kind of collapse anchor for aspects of self.

[23] An Attractor is part of a deeper system that drives surface behaviour, such as the protons and electrons of atoms, the poles of magnets, the sun and earth's centres of gravity, and human interactions.

Much changed in my life. Significantly, I knew that emotional feelings radiated from one person to another. I was having to put words to feelings that I had never experienced before, just as a child does when they are first learning. The difference was that I was doing this as an adult, making my perspective perhaps unique, given my training in physics.

I realised how dissociated from my emotions I had been before; although also how mentally intuitive I had always been. It felt like the feelings had a backdoor signal to my mind, but that I had missed out on the embodying beforehand.

On the basis of this new knowing I invented a new NLP form that I called "Kinaesthetic Gesture Field NLP[24]" (KGF), and together with Sophie Clement[25], I wrote an article on experiencing emotions and applying controls. This was for both allowing the dissociated to safely experience, and the over-associated to learn controls over their experience. Sophie had come from the realm of the over-associated and I from the disassociated.

The essence of KGF is to silently bring your "issue" into the space between your hands, and with gradual hand movements, it evolves and changes on its own, returning the result back whence the issue came. It is free of words, the facilitator is just being with the person, both eyes closed, holding the space for whatever needs to happen, free of thoughts - in the state of being called "no mind".

This was my first experience of perhaps the biggest key to human healing - psycho-activity, where the space becomes "active" or "magical" and everything that then happens changes, imprints or reforms the structure. At the time, this was for me as if the soul had taken over.

Because I had been so dissociated I could empathise with that state of being, and wanted to help to others to re-associate. I therefore became interested in how people dissociate and how best to help others re-associate into the full experience of being human. This was the real inspiration for the onward journey that has produced the Holigral Method.

---

[24] "Kinaesthetic Gesture Field NLP" in Rapport 56

[25] Rapport 57, Some of this article remains in Chapter 17, subsection on dissociation.

1.6 David Grove

The biggest influence that I received in developing Holigral was that of David Grove[26]. I met David at the 2nd Integral NLP Conference on 2nd July 2005. David was famous in certain circles; perhaps notorious would be a better word for him in the world of clinical psychology, where he was always on the cutting edge of new practice.

He was regarded as their "enfant terrible" because of his ability to think outside of the establishment boxes and his willingness to challenge the traditional norms. He learned, practiced and trained others for over thirty years, and during that time gained a worldwide reputation for leading, innovative thinking in psychology.

During that time, David also gained a dedicated following of people who had taken and applied aspects of his work into the wider world. In this community, known as "the clean community", everyone looked to David as the undisputed leader, although he never claimed or wanted such a position.

The members of this tribe were linked by their adherence to David's fundamental principle, which was to seek to be as clean as possible in his interactions with clients.

This meant that the facilitator sought to ensure that all their interactions with the client consisted solely of the client's words and signals, and that they did not intrude any of their comments, suggestions or judgements. In this way, the answers reached by the client came wholly from the client's own system, and were not skewed by input from the facilitator, however well-meaning it might be. Thus, the whole group use the epithet "Clean Language" when they describe what it is that they do.

David came to the conference to give support to presenters of Clean Language, Caitlin Walker in particular. After her seminar at St Mary's Hall, the rector appeared, concerned that shoe marks were scuffing their newly re-polished floor. Josie Drew[27] was on her hands and knees cleaning the floor, and David joined her, cleaning the floor, while everyone else left. That simple act says everything about his generosity of spirit and humility.

---

[26] David Grove, inventor of "Clean Language", and Grovian Metaphor Therapy; a leading non-establishment Clinical Psychologist, trained originally in the arts of Ericksonian Hypnosis.

[27] Josie Drew was one of the conference organisers. She is now Josie Saunders.

He then accompanied Josie back to the Town Hall, and during their conversation it appeared that David and I shared a strong interest in dissociation; at the time we had no idea how strong this was. At the Town Hall, he was re-united with Blossie Mountjoy, my mother, who had attended a number of his events some sixteen to eighteen years earlier.

Then, we were introduced. We spent the greater part of the next few days in a coffee shop talking about dissociation. One of the first things I asked him about were some "missing questions", as I saw it, in the published book on his work - Metaphors in Mind, relating to the inner child. With this, and our mutual interest in dissociation, he made a decision: "As you're already asking the questions and doing the work, I may as well teach you what I know, so you don't make all the mistakes I did" - or some words closely along those lines. What happened next is the real subject of this book[28].

Over the next year, David shared his life's work with me, particularly emphasising "Recovering the child within and without[29]", as this was the main point of exploring dissociation. He also explained his work to my wife, Josie, so that she could be able to teach others.

Our meeting resulted in an explosion of concepts from the world of Physics, Chemistry and Signal Processing, to explain the phenomena observed. Unfortunately, David died in January 2008, and his presence and gifts are missed by many.

The Holigral Method and its underlying model continued to evolve and develop, absorbing insights from working with other gifted individuals, who are credited at the back of the book. All are thanked for their inputs.

---

[28] From a Physics perspective, when two particles interact they become entangled, and what happens with one affects the other; even at distance. When two people meet, depending upon the depth of the emotional engagement and their attractors, they too become entangled, to a lesser or greater extent. Twins, parents and spouses often display this inherent knowing about each other, or their children.

[29] Recovering the "child within and without" refers to the effects of dissociating conditioning, which causes there to be both an inner child that is generally within the body "here but not now", and an external child "neither here nor now", and often an intruded "perpetrator" as part of a defining traumatic moment.

2 A Summary of The Model

The Holigral Method is based upon a model of how reality is constructed by the brain. It broadly assumes that the left side is relational and cognitive in nature, that the right side flows and is intuitive, and that the bridge between these two sides is key to a balanced personal life and a balanced cultural life.

The model for the structure of the left-brain experience is that each human being comprises a personal collective of aspects, each of which is discretely located in space and time.

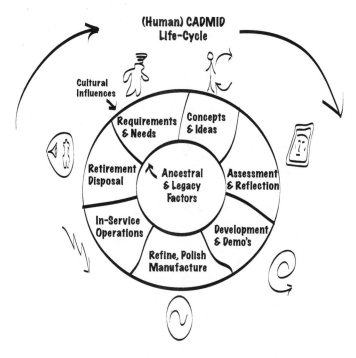

The pattern of the structure of sixes and sevens, expressed as a life-cycle

These aspects are typically separated by six steps in space and six steps in time, although there are reasons for variations in this. The six steps in time or space reflect the six working days of the week, and the aspect of the self is at the seventh, resting.

The model is fractal, meaning it is the same at every scale; within a question, a pattern, a process, and can be seen throughout human experience. For example, it fits engineering design life-cycles and a standard UK government procurement process called the CADMID[30] cycle, as shown in the above diagram.

These aspects are created by defining moments within the personal life, where the structure of the personal collective changes, due to the personal measurement made of the defining moment. They also include a large number of inherited aspects and conditioning through the ancestral DNA. The assumption is "nature and nurture" both play their part.

In a defining moment, there are the aspects of the self dissociated into the environment ("lost life force") and aspects of other people associated into the self ("intruded life force"). The external aspects I call "electrons", and the internal aspects "protons".

After a defining moment, a person attracts new situations and events that reflect the geometry of the original defining moment. The system of the person does this to try to undo the structure; to reclaim the lost life force and to return the intruded life force to someone else. However, all too often, these new events overlay and strengthen the original structure, and life-defining habits emerge.

As well as defining moments, there are defining "epochs". This is how cultural factors influence a person, like osmosis through the skin; almost imperceptible changes or factors that are so ever-present as to be assumed normal. Only time outside of such an environment might make a person aware of such influences. A simple example is the different accents of each town and region in England. The cultural field also experiences defining moments that affect everyone, like the Berlin Wall coming down.

---

[30] CADMID: in response to a Government Requirement, there are six phases in the life-cycle of an equipment: Concepts, Assessments, Development or Demonstration, Manufacture, In-Service and Disposal.

The reason that the association and dissociation happens is because the human is more than the body, and can sense beyond the body boundary. The metaphysical self connects to the body and the world around through the electromagnetic field (e.g. radio waves, light, radar and mobile phone signals). The world around is sensed through this field and also metaphysically. Many people have "eyes in the back of their head", and turn round when someone else is looking at them. This is part of the sixth sense.

In a defining moment a shock interrupts the smooth flow of awareness, and the person has to re-project awareness due to the interruption. The old sensing awareness remains frozen exactly where it was in space and time, and in the same geometric relationship to the body as it was at that defining moment. The person becomes cold - a normal post-shock effect - because of the extra life-force being projected.

The defining moment is undone by re-creating the precise same geometry and awareness flow, reconnecting the own energy and returning the other energy. In practical terms, this involves using patterns of questions and answers to navigate or to re-scale from the present perception to the perception just prior to the defining moment. Navigating from one aspect to another requires crossing the territory in-between.

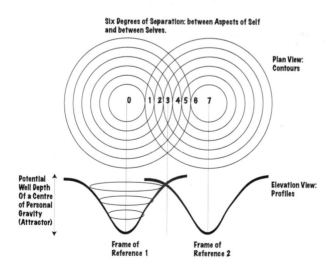

The Structure of Adjacent Attractors

Groups of six questions not only represent six working days but also three degrees of context for each aspect's world view. This comes from the Physics of sampling theory (Nyquist).

The navigation reconnects the selves, and a migration-integration then happens, as the aspect that was frozen in space-time grows up to the present age over a period of a few minutes to hours, sometimes days. Because this process is undoing a measurement, it is called "un-measuring". As the lost energy is returned a person heats up.

The reason why the navigation reconnects the selves is down to aligning the real and the imaginary so that the electromagnetic field is engaged. This is called "psycho-activity", and in such a situation everything that happens changes the structures, as will be explained in more depth, later.

In especially big moments a person can completely disconnect from their previous self and take on a new identity. The boundary to this new self is called "cosmological" because it encompasses the known universe of the self. It is also a boundary that affects the experience through the right side of the brain.

The model for the right-brain is flow-momentum. It has no space or time or relational structures; it is related to movement, moving, and as it is unlimited, it accesses all of space and time because it has no boundaries in space or time. It is also the domain of communing with the other side, and some might say the soul is the identity of the eternal self.

Nonetheless, there are momentum traumas, such as PTSD[31] and body injuries, and methods for undoing them, using question forms that induce flowing.

The interface between the two sides requires exercise to be strengthened. If a person has a cosmological boundary in between them, then this has to first be undone. So question patterns that address left-right-left-right-left-right... will do this naturally.

The types of questions used to undo measurements have to be unrelated to the content of the subject of attention, and completely related to either navigating or flowing. Therefore, they have the form:

---

[31] Post-Traumatic Stress Disorder

"and what could be inside that?"   [navigational, relational]

"and now what is happening?"   [flowing, moving]

These questions are used in patterns of six and seven to undo left-brain structures, so they are repeated, recursively, each new question applying to the last answer:

"and that [last answer] could have come from where?" [six times]

"and what do you know, now?" [once]

If the pattern is indeed fractal, then optimal processes also have to fit the pattern. The first of the fractal processes to be created was called "The Issue Buster", in March 2006. It is now my standard coaching or business-use process to gain clarity upon any subject of attention; simple and quick.

The Issue Buster Process

Step 1: write or draw everything to do with the subject on a piece of paper or whiteboard. Ask six times, "does anything else go on there?"

Ask, "and what do I know, now?"

Step 2: "and what [else] do I know about that?" (6 times)

"and what do I know, now?"

Step 3: "and what does that know about me?" (6 times)

"and what do I know, now?"

Step 4: "and is there anything else about that?" (6 times)

"and what do I know, now?"

Step 5: "and that comes from where?" (6 times)

"and what do I know, now?"

Step 6: "and now what happens?" (6 times)

"and what do I know, now?"

Step 7: "and is there anything else?" (6 times)

"and what do I know, now?"

The design of the process follows the underlying meaning of the days of the week (more on this later), and also addresses the structure of the attractors - below. The self, at 'A', is beholding a subject ('B'). The first step establishes a relationship between 'A' and 'B', just like a meeting or a negotiation. Then, both parties express themselves before the context can be addressed ('C' - literally the space around), and the history, sources and causes established ('D'). Then a new vision can be unrolled, and fleshed out.

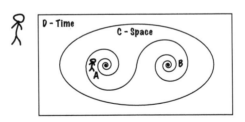

The structure of left-brain aspects[32]

---

[32] The "tissue box" layout, and the notation of ABCD, comes from David Grove. The spiral attractors come from my experience using Chaos Theory in my engineering days. A difference to David's perspective is that I coded 'C' as space and 'D' as time, whereas he coded 'C' as known (the first three steps of six) and 'D' as unknown (the latter three steps).

2.2 The Fractal

The model being fractal, all layers are within each layer, all cycle phases within each cycle phase. The model is a fractal of seven elements, both in cycles and in levels within structures, and the model has the form of the seven days of the week, and also the form of an engineering procurement process (requirements plus the CADMID cycle).

I did not set out to base my model on these patterns; rather these patterns are a reflection of a deep structure that I perceive almost all people use unconsciously to structure reality. In a sense, I might claim this is the structure of whoever designed this universe, or perhaps how it accidentally came to be due to the logic and mathematics of the physics principle of "the path of least resistance"; nature finds the easiest way.

I matched these patterns to the model in hindsight, with the retrospective ability to explain the observations that have come from working with hundreds of people to resolve their life issues. To understand this further, it is worth exploring the nature of the fractal pattern of the days of the week, and how they influence our lives.

Saturday: Antennas and Body

 In engineering and project management terms, this is the Requirements phase, where past cycles are reviewed and the next cycle envisaged. This is the best phase of the cycle to absorb new, wider influences into the next cycle. In structural terms this represents the antennas and physical connection to the world being sensed; the body (physical, emotional, mental and spiritual).

As Chaos Theory relates to much in nature, the starting conditions are all-important, and so the Saturday happenings are of particular relevance. For example, all projects tend to suffer downstream from the false assumptions and errors made in the requirements capture process. In the same way, relationships often founder on small but ultimately significant differences ignored (at their peril) in the starting bliss phase.

Saturday is named after the planet Saturn with its rings, representing the pause and the whole cycle - the Sabbath day of rest. The Roman God Saturn represents the changing year, the transition from one cycle to another, and the feast of the new year (Saturnalia). He is the God of the harvest, and ancient peoples in Northern Europe would harvest and feast on the livestock during the period from the Winter Solstice to New Year. Saturn is also identified with the Greek God Cronos, the god of time. This can be the beginning and/or the end of a cycle; death and rebirth, maybe even reflecting the pause between lifetimes in such a belief system. The remaining six days of the week were also called the children of Cronos in ancient times

Saturday is also the entire cycle and the beginning, the relationship and relating between oneself and the world around, and therefore represents the connection between mind and body (the electromagnetic field) and between the self and the world. The body is the antenna.

Measurement trauma of a "Saturday" type comes from the osmosis of cultural fields and faulty requirements or needs (even if they are mostly inherited from ancestors or past personal cycles).

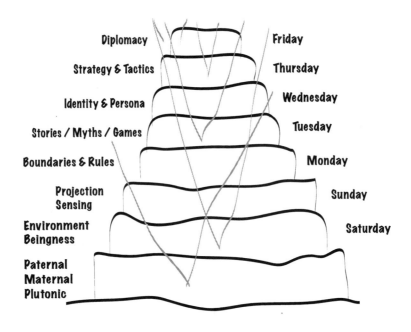

Diplomacy	Friday
Strategy & Tactics	Thursday
Identity & Persona	Wednesday
Stories / Myths / Games	Tuesday
Boundaries & Rules	Monday
Projection Sensing	Sunday
Environment Beingness	Saturday
Paternal Maternal Plutonic	

The deeper the imprinting layer, the greater the impact on the life

From a structural perspective and also the perspective of a developing human being, from conception to death, the model is a pyramid.

The base level is one of beingness in a sea of requirements, which are the energies existing in the world around from the moment of conception. A cell is made from egg (beingness-location) and sperm (drive-momentum), and maybe a third component that some would call the "soul". The DNA in the cell carries the ancestral code in male and female lines, and also the projected energy of the lives of the parents until the point of conception.

In the base level one just experiences what is around, responding with the instinctive coding given in the DNA. The growing body is like the sensor-transducer: the interface between the self and the physical universe that is "the real world". The experience of the beingness is very much that of expand-contract; literally sensing happens as an expanding of awareness and detecting what returns back, just like a radar might operate if it could see in all directions of space and time simultaneously.

This repetitive cycling is the overall pattern, and even within it are coded all the phases of a cycle of simple harmonic motion.

Sunday: Projection and Sensing (Transmitting and Receiving)

 In engineering terms this is the Concept phase of the UK Government's CADMID procurement cycle, and is the systems level of signal detection. It refers to the direction of awareness, focus and the sensitivity to receive signals at all levels of the matrix, in terms of emotional energies.

Sunday, Sontag, represents the sun. Literally the sun radiates; it projects its light out into the universe, giving life in the process. In a meeting or negotiation, the parties will each have to get their prior perceptions, prejudices and projections off their chests before moving on. The human, being one of many, is both a sun and an experiencer of suns; we sense and we radiate.

In a human system and lifecycle this is where incoming and outgoing projections are detected. Normally functioning, this gives a strong intuitive and emotional sensitivity into environments, leading to accurate situational assessment and effective actions.

Overly strong signals or repetitive dangerous signals will concentrate the focus of attention into detecting threats, at the expense of the rest of the environment, maybe even permanently damaging the circuitry and forcing focus onto a restricted range of high-threat signal types. This is readily seen in the rapid scanning of new environments performed by people who have lived in high-threat environments. Just like the highly-threatened radar rapidly scans the near range for threats, so do such people.

People under the perception of high threat to their survival will not focus on the longer term. Thus, for example, politicians cannot truly serve a country when their terms of office are so short compared to the terms of their policy effects.

This second pyramid level is "projection", which is normally experienced inwards from the world around (from the victim or the witness perspectives), but which can also be outwards (from the attacker perspective). The nature of the signals arriving at the body are convolved with the instinctive programming (of the DNA) and structures already in place.

Signals that overload or overly disturb the system will force a structural change in the energy distribution in and around the body, maybe shaping where conscious awareness is focussed and avoided (not focussed).

Monday: Measurement and Adaption; the reflection, boundaries and rules ("The Law")

In engineering terms this is the Assessment phase where the concepts are evaluated, and the systems level of signal measurement. In human lifecycle terms this is where the person adapts by changing their structure and by selecting the nature of what they do measure; the focus of their attention.

Monday, Lundi, Lunes, Montag, represents the moon, which literally reflects the sunlight; sometimes fully, sometimes all in shadow. The moon represents the phases of reflecting on the projections, both the light and the dark aspects; the visible and the unseen. In a meeting, after the parties have had their say, they reflect upon their words and the words of the other parties. Humans both reflect and perceive their reflections from others.

Automated responses are also part of Monday; the reflection in response to other people's projections, and other people's responses to one's own projections likewise.

The Monday trauma is self-inflicted; it is how we change ourselves to adapt or respond to the world. I remember deciding at the age of twelve that I had to "toughen up" to survive at school, and I changed my name to "Steve". Thirty-four years later I undid that, and now I use my full name of "Steven". Understanding the nature of hieroglyphs, I am mightily glad to have the 'n' back.

The typical sayings of a Monday pattern are things like "I did it to myself", or "I cannot control myself". The interactions are between the pronouns of the person, not with the outside world, although they are the consequences of the incoming projections of the Sunday.

Without controls this can lead to social breakdown, and therefore the rules, laws, codes, boundaries and social constraints are applied at this level. It relates to the toddler taming experience. So this is where personal power is expressed, primally through the energetically measured boundaries and their interactions; power is literally seen in the reflection of others' automatic responses.

This third pyramid level is reflection, the moon, where the self adapts to the world around in response, at a structural level. It does this in order to match the world around to survive, to complement the world around to survive, and to generally survive in the best manner for the the self given the circumstances. The body is grown that best fits and adapts to the conditions of the world around, largely defined by the DNA coding but also modified according to other major influences.

Levels two and three (Sunday and Monday) change the structure to optimise sensing and processing of the world in terms of survival and primal threats to existence. These are where fear will be rooted if it is present, as well as all dissociative conditioning. Level three includes boundaries and rules as chosen by the person, whereas level two will express boundaries imposed into or onto the person.

Tuesday: Sorting, Learning and Development, Location, Space; the context

In engineering terms this is the development/demonstration phase, the sorting phase in the intelligence system, and where a human makes learnings about the world; a time for curiosity.

Tuesday, Mardi, Martes, represents Tyr and Mars, the Gods of war, but also in earlier times, the hunt and the land. Tuesday also represents the story landscape and the context. After the parties have disclosed and reflected they can then address the context, acquiring a wider understanding of the whole situation.

Sorting involves matching and recognising similar/different data, and deriving characteristics that will help with identification, for example in characterising the signals of human trauma. The errors made in in sorting create confused characterisations and therefore subsequent mistaken identities. Automated threat responses have false alarms and interfere with properly measuring other signals, which then adversely affects the sorting. Emerging healthily will be morals and understanding of the world around.

Level four of the pyramid represents learning; metaphor, story, myth and games are the media of primary learning. It is a spatial experience where times passes and the story has a flow, the game has a sequence/pattern and lifecycles. There is no structural change in this level; rather learnings can be missed, erroneous or completely wrong, or they might be taken as healthy understanding.

Learning is hierarchical, so we have a pyramidal view of the life-cycle, especially from this perspective:

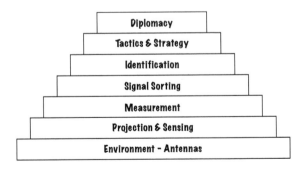

The pattern expressed in the structure of an intelligence system

We can see that, because learning is central to academia, the studies of sociology, psychology and anthropology are likely to be developmental in nature. A perspective aligned with the evolutionary directive assumes that the most highly evolved society is somehow better or superior to the earlier forms of society. If humanity ever again gets as evolved as the code of Ma'At for its basis of law, then perhaps we can claim to be as humane as the Egyptians of five thousand years ago.

Wednesday: Source, Past, Identification, Role, Image, Brand; the metaphor

In engineering terms, this is the Manufacturing phase, where all is refined and polished, ready for service, and products are branded. In human terms, this is where skills are refined; the identity, character or role and mask is acquired. Library identification is the key process in the intelligence system in this phase, and it implies that one has a library of stored identities, and the characteristics of the roles and the associated contextual story. Given the right signal characterisation the identity is easy to understand, as it will reveal the story and the role. Reason, logic and scientific deduction apply.

Wednesday, Mercredi, Miercoles, represents Odin, Woden, Mercury as the messenger of the Gods, so coming from the source. As such it represents understanding the sources and causes of what now is; branding, image, role and identity.

Level five is the domain of archetypes and persona; the roles and the characters played and learned. This develops the personality up to the form required by the world around. In level four (Tuesday) the person resonates with the story prevalent in their life, whereas in level five they choose, adopt or become the role required to best survive or fit into the wider story or stories being played out in their local world.

If you take the trouble to analyse a problem using these five stages, you will attain a comprehensive understanding by the time the Wednesday is finished. From surveying the whole context, the causes and the interests of the parties, a way ahead can be divined that works best for all, which leads into Thursday. That is the Issue-Buster process in action.

Thursday: Tribes, Tactics, Strategy, Social World, Future, Sequence, Order

This is the engineering and human In-Service phase, where products are used, services supplied, and habits are played out. It is the unrolling of time, forward; direction, momemtum-flow, operations, logistics and overall the central vibration of business and warfare.

Thursday, Jeudi, Jueves, is Thor's day, Jove's day, the God of lightning - literally signalling the direction, rollout out the vision, the future, the strategy or tactics to be employed. This is where tactics and strategies are played out as games, scripts and story action, working in the tribes of "us and them"; "the enemy of my enemy is my friend". In this level the persona learns how to run with their own pack and the games of tactics and strategy.

Thursday being the flow, there is little to do but to play out the games set up in the previous phases and layers. There are maintenance activities, mid-life-upgrades, and habits. To end them, one proceeds to Friday - retirement.

Friday: Hindsight, Observer, Retirement, Death; a healthy perspective

This is the engineering Retirement phase and the level of diplomacy after all the action has played out. It is the applause after the performance, and where people can let go of habits or learnings to make space for what comes next; death, bereavement and equanimity. This is where right understanding takes pride of place, where mourning, bereavement and grief have their full play.

Friday, Vendredi, Viernes, is Freya-Venus day. Beauty is indeed in the eye of the beholder, when this pattern is worked with. Friday therefore represents the observer; after conflicts, the UN Observers go in to oversee the peace.

Level seven is about realising the self into a "we" paradigm; true diplomacy, where the forms of influence are entailments and deals are "everyone wins". Almost no-one makes it to this level, and those who do are unlikely to be understood for their actions, as altruism is not in the nature of any levels below, save for the martyr archetype.

The Week

Around this pattern of seven are three influences of ancestral masculine, feminine and cultural legacy and background: Uranus, Neptune and Pluto representing the guardianship of the other side. So levels two and three are those of physics, levels four and five are metaphor and story, and levels six and seven are about sequence and foresight, prediction, anticipation, based upon understanding all that has passed before and the present signals.

The river bed and banks shape the flow, and the flow shapes the river bed and banks; both are required to define the river, but all the influence and information lies in the boundary layers, according to fluid mechanics.

Coming back full circle to Saturday, it is the whole relationship and the interaction; the body is that which interfaces the self to the world, to the "matrix" of human experience, and all the chaos and structures emerge from the starting conditions within the relating.

2.3 The Right-Brain

In tandem with this structure is also the flow, which is like the momentum equivalent of space-time structures of seven. In this alternative flow world there is no structure; just an eternity as flow has no beginning, no end, no location in space or time. Flows can be in a kind of parallel where they influence each other in a flowing adjacency, and flows can be structured into cycles.

Related to the flow is what I call "the field". This is my name for slowly changing cultural influences which affect the person, although to most appearances they are eternal as they are taken like constants which change so slowly as to be virtually imperceptible.

The field-flow is what people who live in the margins of society experience, as a rule. They have insufficient material interest to bother competing for resources like the left-brain dominant majority, They will be highly intuitive and artistically skilled compared to normals who conform to the space-time world of rules and regulations. They will be more in tune with animals and plants, and practical crafts, and have little time for the written word. They certainly would not bother to read this book, knowing most of this intuitively, already.

Measurements made in momentum are flows, like a bubbling stream, better expressed as "moving experiencing flowing" - for example, "story-telling", "excusing", "justifying", "rationalising", "qualifying" and "complaining". There is no space or time, no beginning and no end to a momentum measurement-experience. This is what some people call "the now"; quite funny as this word is a space-time description of "moving-being-experiencing-nowing-flowing".

Native American, Russian and Hungarian are languages that more effectively (than occidental languages) use both principles in communicating; reflecting the more nomadic nature of their cultural heritages. The two brain hemispheres fundamentally address these two principles, and the strength of bridge between them reflects the ease with which a person is combining both in their daily life.

A more complete experience (a complete experiencing) is both location and momentum, but also not precisely either; and un-measured. A typical (normal) adult human being is the result of thousands of measurements, and they communicate these measurements through every movement, gesture, posture, sound, word and deed, through their clothing, home, family, possessions, hobbies and jobs.

Compare the different effect of these two questions, in relation to a problem or a focus of attention:

"and, what, do you, know, about, that?"
(Sat, Weds, Mon, Tue, Thu, Sun) (Answer = Fri)   (Left-Brain)

"and, that, you know, what, about [that]?"
(Sat, Sun, Mon, Tue, Wed, Thu, [Fri])   (Right-Brain)

These questions, and the responses, show the difference from being entranced into the left-brained, lexic pattern or being in the right-brained, nonlexic flow. As the questions progress, so the effects diverge.

People of "the flow" find it far easier to answer the latter question, and in so doing, they get the complete revelation of the subject in their mind, like a 3D movie playing in their mind. People who are more cognitive-relational will

44

respond better to the former question and benefit from the six iterations of that question.

After working with Julie Sellars, a dyslexic, and also the learning difficulties coordinator at a college in Sussex, it emerged that the nonlexics, as we prefer to call them, are mostly right-brain, and can rapidly acquire reading skills once deprogrammed from a left-brained way of teaching-learning.

This insight first came because I met a Romanian in December 2009, and I wanted to translate the questions accordingly. The word order differences made me curious, and I actually preferred the English words in Romanian order. Something "more" was happening; the questions enabled a complete revelation in one go; no sixes, no iterations.

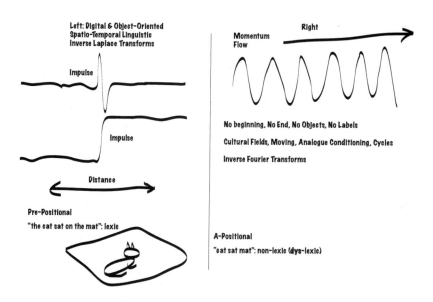

The left and the right side of measurement

The left-side, above, normally relates to instantaneous traumas that happen in defining moments, and the right-side usually relates to flows: stories, physical activities and habits, like excuses, justifications, reasons, analysis, complaints and justifications. These stereotypical allocations of right and left are not true in all cases, but the point is to show that these two different aspects of reality relate to fundamental mathematics and physics, and to the brain.

The structure of questions and their delivery is vastly different between cognitive and momentum questions, as the delivery has to match the form of the measurement system being engaged in the un-measuring process (next diagram). Below are examples of the three main forms of questions:

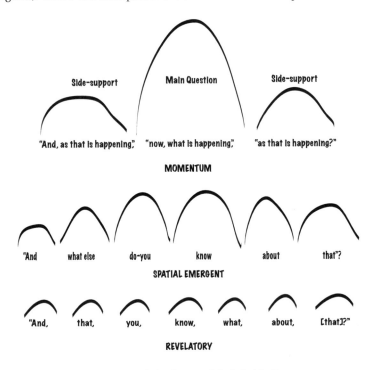

"Beauty is in the eye of the beholder"

The momentum form of questions is like these:

"and now what is happening?"

"and-ing now-ing what-ing is-ing happening?"

"and as that is happening, now what is happening, as that is happening?"

This pattern is repeated for as long as required, until the starting conditions are resolved and the client is free of them.

Looking back at essay writing, and reports or proposals, I noticed that they take the form of the inside-out issue-buster (1-45362-7: Sat-Tues-Wed-Mon-Thu-Sun-Fri), because the written word has to write out the picture, the beauty, in a totally different way to the direct experience. The direct experience is Saturday to Friday; the pattern of emergence.

Then I realised that the old spoken English was in the 1-7 form (Saturday through to Friday), but that as written English spread and fixed the form and usage of the language, so it fed back into spoken English, and now mostly people speak inside-out in form; it has become the norm.

But, the old form brings an experience beyond words, beyond essays; it reveals Venus in all her glory. The beholder is the mirror, the moon, and the glory beheld is the sun. The word sequences below are unusual for a reason; try them. Below is a useful pre-frame for the more lexic members of society:

> "The questions are unusual in structure, different to written English or modern spoken English, but they are in the form of old spoken English. Let the question have its effect, give yourself time for the answering experience to emerge, and you might just get something unexpectedly wonderful ..."

Issue-Busting 2: Revelation

"and, [problem/goal], your attention, bring to."

"and, that, you know, what about?"

"and, you, that knows, what about?"

"and, anything else, you sense, about that?"

"and, that, you sense, comes, from where?"

"and, as knowing, now what is happening, as knowing?

"and, with you, happens what, now?"

The Hare and the Tortoise

The left and the right brains are reflected well in popular culture as the tortoise and the hare, respectively. Neither understand the other at all well, and there are very few people who have both in balance. The reason for this stems back long into the past, to events at least 3200 years ago, but the effects are now manifest in the world's structures and laws.

How does a hare talk to a tortoise, when their worlds are so different? The tortoise rules the land with process and law, with power and social hierarchy. The hare wanders and explores, and has little interest in the status and material possessions of the tortoise. The hares live "literally" in the margins. It is time to realise the value of autism, nonlexia and those locked up in the madhouses, and to integrate the two cultural perspectives of the hare and the tortoise.

Because of the languaging, combining a left-right pattern of questions gives the full experience. The difference between this approach and the Issue Buster 2 is that this time the momentum principle is added, expanding the vision at each stage, and then the understanding is related in the third question.

The pattern is "revelation, right brain (left foot), left brain (right foot)"; a triple form, combining the above process with a left-right, relational, flowing doublet. This process is "flowing object-move-object-move". "That" is the subject of attention.

The pattern also exploits the physics of all the information being at the boundary. The boundary is the bridge between the two halves of the brain; the interface between the two systems of perception; the relational, cognitive, object-oriented, locational left brain and the momentum-flow, experiential right brain. Through the switching between these two aspects of perception, they start to merge, and the complete experience begins. Welcome home!

Integrated Issue-Busting Process (3)

And, problem or goal, your attention, bringing to.

And, that, you know, what about?
a) and as knowing, now what is happening, as knowing?
b) and, knowing, happens what, now?
And, you, that knows, what about?
a) and as that knowing, now what is happening, as that knowing?
b) and, that knowing, happens what, now?

And, anything-else, you sense, about that?
a) and as sensing anything-else, now what is happening, as sensing anything-else?
b) and about-that, you're sensing, anything else?

And, that, you sense, comes, from where?
a) and as sensing coming from, now what is happening, as sensing coming from?
b) and, sensing from there, happens what, now?

And knowing, you doing what, now?
a) and, as knowing, doing, now what is happening, as knowing, doing?
b) and, with you, happens what, now?

If a person is seriously conditioned into the left-brain they may not make much sense of this pattern. In this case they are best served by reverting to the first Issue Buster.

2.4 The Eternal Self and Cosmological Boundaries

The bigger defining moments have been defined as "cosmological". The structures of cosmological defining moments create a complete separation of consciousness between the past and present selves, and it is not beyond the bounds of possibility that the separate personalities of a schizoid could be held apart by such structures. These aspects can be completely unaware of each other.

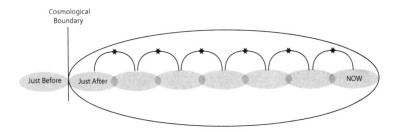

Cosmological perspective (the shadowed ellipses are the perceptual worlds; those in between are like the intermediate floors of the spiral staircase of a building.)

A cosmology is a person's present self's most global world view. It holds metaphysical worlds (typically six), and comprises the entire client's metaphysical system relating to life. Typically seven interim perceptual worlds away is the cosmology preceding the current one.

This cosmology literally comprises the fundamental belief system of a client. Generally a client has no access to knowledge outside of their present cosmology. It represents their understanding of the universe, no less.

Before (outside of) the creation of this cosmology lies a real-scaled memory world of life before – life before a trauma or a defining moment in life. Within the set of worlds also lies the polar opposite of the operating belief or behaviour or identity.

One example client found that their present world went back through the six perceptual worlds to a seventh containing their defining moment, where they associated into a scientific mind set as a result of a science fiction book they were reading. Literally they had dissociated into the book, and therefore had an amazing understanding of cosmology. Their previous cosmology was the world of the small child; magical and without so many cares.

Chaining perceptual worlds, eventually one reaches a place (generally at six or seven perceptual worlds), where a "planar bisection" delimits a cosmology. 'A' has no knowledge beyond this place until "adjacency" is achieved at the final 'D' boundary.

Around 'D' is the world of the cosmological self before the present one, and the boundary to that is therefore called cosmological. Literally this previous self is the maker of the present self - its "God", as it were. Continuous memory does not pass through such boundaries, but the navigation processes to be described do successfully negotiate them.

The spaces delimiting the boundaries of a cosmology are real-scaled and separated by six strangely scaled[33] worlds. A planar bisection is a special case whereby an entirely different cosmology is held. There are no memories of what is the other side until the boundary is explored and crossed. So it is also the "cosmological boundary".

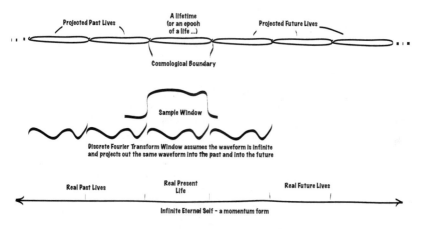

The difference between REAL and PROJECTED past lives, between real and projected earlier selves

---

[33] Strangely scaled: the intermediate worlds, where the geometry is not the same as the real world; its scale is therefore "strange". This is one of David Grove's terms.

51

The Fourier Transform is a way of moving between a frequency representation and a time representation of something. The Discrete Fourier Transform is used to practically measure frequencies from time series. It puts a window around the measurement, and assumes the frequency exists in the past and the future in the same way as within the window of measurement.

It is the appropriate way to understand the momentum selves and changes in frequency due to defining moments. The defining moments make the frame of the windows, limiting the experience of frequencies, and make assumptions about the past epochs reflecting the present epoch.

Given this momentum understanding, the corollary is the infinite present: nowing - momentum. The corollary of this is the existence of the eternal self. Breaking the cosmological boundaries of the selves reveals the real past epochs, changing the present perception, and this is observable and measurable with clients. The model being fractal, this applies at every scale.

As defining moments occur they cut off the present self from the past momentum self; these are the really big boundaries, the cosmological ones that can leave no memory even of the past before the moment, such as the difference between present memory, photograph memory and "parental stories about you" memory.

Adolescence is one such chemical boundary, which partly explains how young male drivers can behave so badly in relation to the children they only recently were. Many adults forget what it is like to be children. Another corollary, is that all momentum selves go to the dawn of time and beyond, and therefore they are all "God", all the same being.

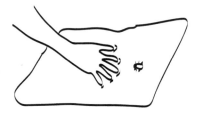

We are all one, even if it may not appear so.

A being living only on the table will not experience the whole, but rather will perceive the fingers as different, unconnected entities.

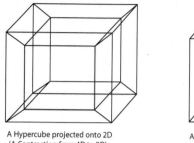

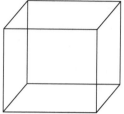

A Hypercube projected onto 2D
(A Contraction from 4D to 2D)

A Cube projected onto 2D
(A contraction from 3D to 2D)

The Eternal Universe

A corollary of the eternal self and a fractal model though, is that the universe must also be designed the same way. The present mind cannot conceive of a prior universe except of the form of the present one. The present universe has this big bang microwave background signal, but it comes from all directions as if there is no "other origin". The answer, in my analysis, is because "here" is the origin. The past universe echoes in the big bang are actually the "splashback" of its creation from the nowing, and the last big universe re-measuring was the Galilean separation from "God", circa 1450.

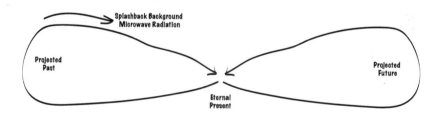

Cosmic splash-back; the echoes of "the big bang" moment of creation

There was a smaller, later shift - relativistic, about one hundred years ago, with relativity and quantum changing the scientific rules, but essentially it's the same "universe". However, it is now projected out to about fourteen billion years old at the last estimate; projected out from the now-ing, limited by the scientific world view, which is only about 500-550 years old. The same diagrams used for the self now apply to the universe; past ones and future ones are projected beyond this one because the mind within this one cannot conceive of the one created before the mind was.

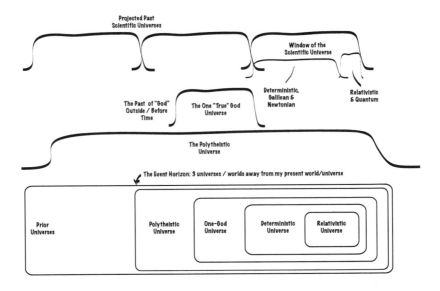

Sequential and/or nested universes of creation

Luckily, the eternal self can penetrate this boundary and see the universe of before, and before that. The prior universe was that of the "One God" projection, created about 3200 years ago[34], with its own "projected" origin of about 10,000 BCE in present parlance.

Perhaps we now have an explanation for the real persecution of heretics and nonbelievers; the need to erase competing belief systems, which in effect could destroy the universe of the said "One God". Thus, the enforcers

---

[34] This cosmological boundary is addressed in another book, entitled "The Return of the Gods".

devised the particularly nasty death by purification by fire and forced the recantation - to literally un-spell the heretical spell.

The universe before that of the "one, true God" was the polytheistic one, and there is presently no counting on that, but the Greek histories and tales tell of four ages of man: Golden, Silver, Bronze and Iron. So, I could postulate that we are at the end of the sixth age of mankind, and about to enter a pause; a rest of ages, the seventh.

The Egyptians also tell of the wrath of Sekhmet[35], and most cultures share the flood myth and of a lost, "golden" civilisation. As sea levels rose, and civilised areas flooded, did the end of the last Ice Age end one of these ages? The question though, is whether the age of titans and before is the antecedent of the age of the Gods containing these four ages of mankind, or whether they represent some other ages of experience; such as ages before mankind - dinosaur and so on.

2.5 The Field

Another component of the model is "the field" - patterning of energy densities and attractors developed through the aeons of life, exhibited as cultural patterns and codes. This field holds the cultural equivalent of the single human being; what Jung called "the collective unconscious".

An even more complete experience would also include the entire group-collective consciousness. The group field mostly changes slowly and imperceptibly to the lifetimes of people, but sometimes change happens quicker, like 9/11, and an indelible mark is made on society.

Something that has always been true in a person's life is like a permanent, unconscious field, ever-present. If a person has never left their country or never learned a foreign language fluently, they may not realise that the very language we use limits our ability to think and perceive. Things like language and social codes are the local cultural field. Older, deeper things like archetypal roles, such as Little Red Riding Hood, are common to wider cultures but nonetheless still part of the cultural field.

About two hundred years ago the spoken English language underwent a shift that one can see in the word order of, for example, the poetry of Sir

---

[35] Sekhmet punished the people for disrespecting Ra as he aged and became decrepit.

Walter Scott. Before then, the natural flow of spoken words was poetic and measured to create an effect of "beauty in the eye of the beholder". The pre-lexic and nonlexic person finds the written word so vastly inefficient compared with the forms of direct revelation and knowing available to these "marginalised" people.

Field Changes

What happened in Sir Walter Scott's time was that the written word started to overtake the spoken word as a form of learning, and then people started to speak in the same order as written. There are still some country areas where the older form is used in everyday, local conversation. This shift of word sequence has resulted in a general loss of intuition and the marginalising of those who refuse the lexic belief system, gradually but consistently over two hundred years. Finally, the rebellions of autism and nonlexia are the symptoms of a society realising a sickness.

I believe it takes about one hundred and fifty to two hundred years for a cultural cycle to complete; six to seven generations. To understand today's problems, I believe that culturally one must understand history, at least as far back as the days before Moses.

The big field changes are things like "the One God myth, circa 1200 BCE", "science splitting from religion circa 1500 CE", and "from determinism to relativism circa 1900 CE".

Beyond

Chunking up from the single human being, one can see the layers of metaphysical creation reflect the same pattern. Typically, the perception of "God" proves to be the projection of a self, later than the primal self of the person.

So far, I'm talking about one hundred percent of the clients, who have navigated far enough, having each experienced the same realisation about the so-called "One God". They have not been led to this conclusion; many students did not make it this far, and those who did have made their realisations independently of my beliefs.

As opposed to some "cults" who intrude a reality at the point of greatest vulnerability[36], the point is to stay clean and have people discover their realisations for themselves, from their own, personal awareness.

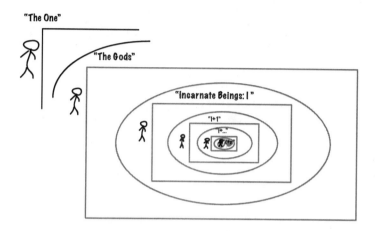

Nested layers of beingness

The "trick" is to go past this projection of "God" and to connect to the real wider energies around; the realm of "the real Gods", not projections from a constrained world view.

2.6 Applying the Model

Having introduced the model overall, but not having addressed the underlying Physics, next follows example processes from each of the phases of the cycle.

The intelligence system is one of the most refined forms of technological development. It is also an application that is modelled on human intelligence, and on solving similar problems in terms of understanding and

---

[36] The ideas of aliens, reptiles, guru, etc. are intruded at the time of energetic porousness.

interpreting environments in order to inform decisions for the best course of action. It has many levels and layers of feedback, which will mirror the layering of the designers and users of these systems. From top to bottom, these are:

Intelligence System	**Environmental Context**
Sensors / **Sensor Functions** / **Sensor Management**	**Projecting** & **Sensing**
Measurement / **Object Parameters** / **Direction, range, velocity.**	**Boundaries** & **Rules**
Signal Sorting / **Clustering, Associating** / **Tracking, Sense-Making**	**Stories** & **Games**
Situation Awareness / **Pattern Recognition,** / **Identification, Matching**	**Roles** & **Identity**
Tactical / **Threat Assessment,** / **Deployment, Action**	**Tactics**
Strategic / **Planning, Diplomacy** / **Collaborative**	**Diplomacy** & **Death**

A set of systemic levels

This model is mapped used to contextualise and make sense of the experiences and the processes related to the different levels, kinds and phases of the human experience and trauma.

Different Kinds of Processes

Depending upon the phase of the life-cycle, so the nature of a "trauma" changes. The dissociative structural traumas[37] relate to the Sunday and Monday phases only, where one is impacted by an external projection, or one changes oneself in order to adapt.

The other phases allow for simpler and easier interventions, such as changing a learning or refining an understanding, dissolving a habit, and retiring something obsolete.

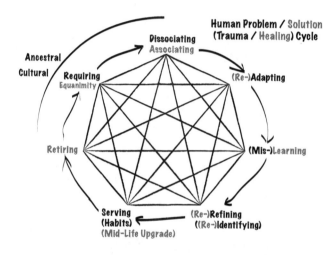

Seven different forms of trauma and intervention

The Septagram shows the twenty-one links of influence between the phases. Typically one only sees the perimeter connections in action (cause and effect).

---

[37] These are the traumas that create attractors and separations, as already described in the model. I distinguish them here from the other kinds of traumas, which are more minor in nature and more easily healed.

3 The Body's Antenna

3.1 Introduction

The first level of the intelligence system involves the sensor functions: radiating and receiving energy, managing antenna patterns to direct energy and receptivity[38]. This aspect interacts directly with the environment.

Because it is the most primal, environmental aspect, this is probably what develops first in a human being; radiating, managing and sensing energy. The sensing includes the own body: learning the control of the body through the nerves and and sensory feedback. The mind-self learns how to coordinate the body and use it as its access into "the physical world". Until the basic sensor functions are controlled and operable, not much more can be done with the system. As focus is controlled, so awareness can be guided.

The nature of the interface between the self and the body is addressed first, as this is the key to understanding how fundamental human change is effected. To understand this, there are some basic principles to consider.

The Observer

 For one hundred years now, we have known that "the observer affects the experiment[39]". In other words, something witnessed or measured or experienced with judgement is changed by the very nature of the observing.

---

[38] Receptivity is the gain of the receiving antenna in different directions when it is not isotropic. This can be different to the gain of the transmitting antenna, which can also be anisotropic.

[39] This is called "Heisenberg's Uncertainty Principle", after the man who discovered it. It also explains why we cannot both measure location and momentum accurately in the same measurement; we can measure one or the other accurately or both approximately. It is also a reflection of the human brain, with two sides, one for object-oriented, relational interaction, and the other for flow and momentum experience.

This is not a principle that just applies in particle physics experiments, but also in the world of human interaction. For example:

- ☉ Walk down the High Street looking at the back of a person and they may well turn around and look back. There is a connection. In the UK, females seem generally more responsive to such looking, but there is no inherent gender primacy.

- ☉ Having an observer present during a performance review meeting changes the ways both the manager and the team member act.

- ☉ Watching a parent in a potentially child-abusive situation can stop the parent from abusing - at least in public. Cameras change the way people act in public places. In the absence of a belief in a real God, or metaphysical watcher, we have created our own physical "big brother" to compensate for the darker side of human nature.

- ☉ What others might perceive, think or do affects how we behave - this is both social conditioning and part of the nature of our universe.

The basis of modern physics is quantum, and the basis of quantum physics is two principles: those of uncertainty and measurement. The Uncertainty Principle says that either something can be measured accurately as a location (in space and time) or in a movement (momentum) but both cannot be measured accurately at the same time. To understand something fully, one needs to know it from both perspectives; both location and momentum. It is not fully either, and is approximately both.

3.2 Real and Imaginary

The Ancient Greeks based their understanding of the universe upon whole numbers, numbers that we call integers: "1, 2, 3" and so on. About 300 years ago a French mathematician called De Moivre invented the concept of complex numbers. These are numbers with two components: one part real and the other part imaginary. Initially these complex numbers were used to find answers to equations that did not have real answers - a kind of purely intellectual mathematical curiosity - see the graph, below.

This graph has no crossing points on the x-axis, and so there is no real solution to the problem of finding such crossing points. For another example, if I were to ask you to show me "minus two bananas", you cannot. Even negative numbers are imaginary in nature, although they can feel very real on a bank balance.

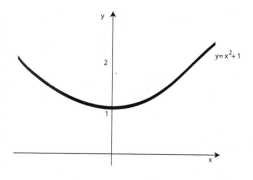

$$y = x^2 + 1$$

About 1900 CE, Einstein began his work on relativity, again using real and imaginary numbers (and dimensions), to represent space-time. About the same time, quantum physicists used the same complex mathematics to create equations that reflect the nature of the physics of the very small. So, we have real and imaginary dimensions covering all scales of reality, from the very small to the very large. Our personal scale of reality is also both real and imaginary.

About 1850 CE, James Clerk Maxwell used these complex numbers to define the laws of electromagnetism. Now, all radio, laser, radar and electronic circuits are designed using this form of mathematics. Mobile phones have components in them that have real and imaginary properties which affect the real and imaginary aspects of the radio waves that the phones transmit and receive.

Electromagnetic waves (radio, light) travel as photonic[40] wave-packets[41], illustrated below, literally corkscrewing through the real-and-imaginary space (and perceived time).

---

[40] Photonic: a photon is the name for a single light-wave-particle; it is both a wave and a particle with neither location nor momentum fully measured.

[41] A wave packet is a wave that does not go on forever, measurably, although it does infinitesimally exist in all of space and time; it is primarily localised in a region of space and time.

Real-only view of a wave-packet   **Complex view of a wave-packet**

The electromagnetic field seems to be an interface between the real and the imaginary, based upon the mathematics and also upon the logic of considering that nothing else apparently does this. While many scientists are very happy to have the mathematical convenience of imaginary numbers, they tend to be very unhappy with the consequences – in fact, they tend to deny them.

The consequence of our scale of reality being real and imaginary is that we also have real and imaginary components. The real components are the physical body and the chemicals within it. The imaginary components are those things which cannot be "measured" by physical equipment: our minds, spirit and emotions. And, electricity (or electromagnetism) is the interface that provides the communication between the real and the imaginary parts of us.

My evidence for this comes from considering what would have to be true in order to explain the phenomena of: coma, paralysis, phantom limb experiences, mind control of devices through electromagnetic fields (below), sight (below), experience, mind, imagination, ghosts, spirits, questioning "what is the emergent property differentiating an alive body and a dead one, and one in a coma?", a process that reveals one's physical projection and the collapse of projection in near-death, and the muscle tensions of awake versus sleeping people.

The mind influences the body through this field, and the body returns signals from the real world to the mind through it. Electrical equipment affects your mind and emotions, and your mind and emotions affect electrical equipment.

If you choose a low-signal-strength location you can turn your mobile phone reception on or off at will, with practice. Remote car locking devices have significantly longer range if you hold them to your head when you operate them. Try it. This is because your body is an antenna; it picks up electrical signals and it also radiates them.

Of particular interest is the brain, where electrical signals from the senses become patterns of waves. These patterns in turn become the sensed "three-dimensional through time" experience that the self has in the mind-field.

The mechanism to understand brain waves, neuronal intensities and distributions is to think in terms of chaotic attractors, where the time series of optic nerve electrical impulses are converted into 3D relationships, and the locations reveal the attractors. The peak of neuronal intensities reveals a mapping into the strong attractors in the world around.

How do you see? It is all very well to claim that vision is an emergent property of the brain, but how to explain the real-time 3D visual experience as if you were looking at a 3D cinema? Is it at all logical to suggest that this experience really happens due to distributed electrical potentials and firing/non-firing neurons throughout the brain?

The brain provides the physical mechanism for transferring the visual (and other sensory) information into electromagnetic form which then, perhaps, enables the imaginary mind/spirit to perceive it, through how it has distributed in the brain-space.

In particular, the neurons distributed throughout your body enable the mind-body communication. You have as many neurons in your stomach as your brain stem, and there are neurons in your heart and anus. And when someone looks they will find neurons in hands, fingers, feet and toes; indeed throughout the body.

So, what if the proof of the existence of dark matter, spirit, "God", or mind has been sitting in front of our scientific noses for four hundred years, but our belief systems have precluded our ability to notice this simple evidence?

As everything is actually complex, it is highly unlikely that something is either entirely real or entirely imaginary, although some things could be mostly real or mostly imaginary, and other things will fluctuate in terms of how real or imaginary they are. The real and imaginary axes of a complex space are infinitesimally small aspects of that whole space. And yet, both are necessary for life. What if the realm of imaginary life were more teeming, or even more real, than the physical?

Human Measurement

A human measurement is made as both a real and an imaginary experience, either in location or in momentum, and so the laws of complex mathematics apply. The imaginary dimension is at right-angles to the real dimension.

By applying the inverse to the measurement, it can be undone; for example $2 \times \frac{1}{2} = 1$ (2 and ½ are the inverse of each other). In complex mathematics, there are "Hermitian Matrices[42]" with the useful property of being "self-inverse", meaning that the process of creating a measurement is the same as the process of destroying a measurement - "un-measuring".

The movement of human awareness may well exhibit Hermitian effects. As awareness re-touches the time and space of a past measurement, it is unmeasured, as if it never was. In a measurement, human attractors are created that result in repeating patterns of events. There is a reason for this, that explains the mechanism, but first we need more concepts explained.

The only real matrix that is self-inverse is called the identity matrix[43]. This is quite funny, for me, because it equates to the only real experience of having no opposite being an identity-state of "oneness". I imagine that a total dissociation could be considered the opposite, though.

3.3 Relativity

In relativity, every point of perception is a unique frame of reference, and time behaves differently in each location. For me, every point is conscious, and also unique. So what? How is this useful? If you coincide your real and your imaginary, then some very powerful change becomes possible.

By placing the content of a problem (something imaginary) at the same focus as the physical eye focus, the real and the imaginary are aligned in terms of moving consciousness; this is what is called "psychoactive space". This

---

[42] A Hermitian Matrix is self-inverse, and only the identity matrix or complex matrices can be Hermitian. I was asked why or how I linked this concept. Basically, I was looking for equivalent mathematics or physics that related to the experience of the work of David Grove. David Grove asked me to, and so I continued to do this.

[43] Identity matrix, simplified two by two: {{1,0},{0,1}}. See wikipedia.

means that operations, such as turning, act like a light-wave in space-time - they corkscrew through planes of perception, navigating and permanently changing perception accordingly. For this, I designed a machine, called the Ark Angle, which enables this to be done efficiently and fast - below.

The prototype Ark Angle

The essence of all permanent, profound, human change work requires the space to become "psychoactive", which is the same effect as aligning the real and the imaginary.

So there is a mathematics and a physics for affecting the mind, using the body and mind, together. Body-only or mind/emotion-only approaches cannot affect the system as powerfully as an approach that combines both.

The Ark Angle machine can rotate on any desired axis of rotation (roll, pitch and yaw), including rotating all three axes simultaneously. This enables the undoing of human "measurements" by applying the idea of Riemann surfaces in relation to rotation in complex space.

When a space becomes "psychoactive", then movement in that space causes changes to the structure of experience of the person for whom the space is psychoactive. Setting up the right starting conditions makes a space psychoactive, as do hypnotic inductions (the basis for traditional NLP) and hallucinatory drugs. This means the mathematics of complex numbers and complex spaces then applies.

A psychoactive space is one where a person perceives something imaginary at a particular location or with a particular movement, overlaid on the real world. In the person's experience they may or may not see the imaginary thing, but they will know where it is.

So, for example, once a person is engaged with an imaginary "spider" ten feet away from them, simply by rotating themselves six times a fear of the spider can be made to literally disappear. What has happened in this instance is that the rotation has been made in a complex space, not just a real space.

Also, in the complex space the rotation does not return them to the same location. Rather, it is like being on a metaphysical spiral staircase – the person has literally moved to a parallel reality (like moving to a different floor of a building) where they no longer experience the fear. This is also effectively how light moves – corkscrewing its way through space by rotating in a complex space with both real and imaginary components. Strange, but true.

We can literally rotate our way out of trauma. Recall a few old wives sayings, like "He's taken a turn for the worse/better", "He's gone round the bend", "She's got a screw loose", "She's got her head screwed on", "I got out of the wrong side of the bed this morning", and recall the whirling Dervishes. Maybe, just maybe, there is something to turning-spinning-rotating-gyrating?

3.4 Using the Ark Angle

The machine has its own language, relating to balance and the interaction of angular momentum[44] between the axes of rotation. Rather than the action you would expect of a gyroscope or fairground whirlygig, the purpose here is to rotate or move very slowly, as a rule, so that there is time for the awareness to search out the directions and update. If the rotation is too

---

[44] Angular momentum is the rotational counterpart to momentum, and it is conserved in the absence of external torque.

fast then the psychoactivity will be broken.

There is a counterbalance to largely address centre of gravity variations between clients. Once this is compensated, the machine is ready to move according to the client's body need, which is in the directions of least resistance. If turning a direction becomes hard work the force is transferred to another axis which releases the resistance.

As the changes occur mentally, so the directions and resistances change physically, perhaps due to changes in muscle tension changing the balance of the client.

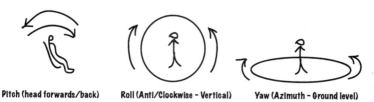

Pitch (head forwards/back)   Roll (Anti/Clockwise - Vertical)   Yaw (Azimuth - Ground level)

The machine can rotate or rock or prescribe solid angles using combinations of yaw, pitch and roll. Yaw is azimuthal, rotating horizontally; pitch is head-forwards or head backwards, and roll is in the vertical plane, clockwise and counterclockwise. The azimuthal yaw is made by the wheels on the legs of the machine, rotating round the trackway. The pitch is controlled by the pitch wheels, and the roll is performed by rotating the main ring.

In complex mathematics, a rocking motion is the same as a circular motion, as they both describe an underlying mechanism of "Simple Harmonic Motion"[45]. Vibration is perhaps an easier way of understanding this. Waves at the seaside have this motion, and as they break you can see the underlying broken circle of the motion as the sea floor rises up to interfere with the rolling wave. This is why big sea waves are called "rollers".

So, the machine can be used in complete cycles, in rocking motions in one axis, in rocking motions over two or three axes, or it can be used in discrete pointing directions and body postures.

---

[45] Simple harmonic motion is circular motion projected into waves or cycles or periodicities.

One interesting result of mixing pitch and roll was to find that the cause of seasickness seems to be related to whether a person's mother had nausea during the pregnancy. The Ark Angle appears to undo this cause of seasickness. At present we do not know if there are other causes, but it is worth wondering if this also relates to space sickness and its cure.

The machine has proven a marvel in relation to dissociations and intrusions that have happened in the womb, during conception, rooting of the fertilized egg, birth, cot, pram, push-chair and pre-crawling traumas. The machine accesses body postures and angles that relate to those of the foetus in a way it is really not possible otherwise, and therefore can re-trigger and thus undo those defining moments.

Naming the Process

I decided that David Grove's original name of *"Spinning"* implied something dizzy-making, which is not reflected in client symptoms. *"Turning"* better describes the motion. However, the whole "direction, turning and accessing information" experience can become sophisticated and complicated.

This is reflected in the development of radar technology which, as a creation of the mind of man, is a mirror of man's mind. Radar systems and how they work relate intimately and accurately to how human beings manage their personal situation awareness. For every direction of eye access, there are some parameters, which are largely independent of each other:

- Two angles (azimuth and elevation) - conceptually though, people may only perceive this as one angle.
- There are also the subtleties of orientation angle of whatever is at the place of focus and the body orientation and posture of the perceiver.
- Distance(s) from the eye(s) to the area(s) of focus.
- A time (present or past or imaginary future, very recent or long time or multiple overlays), and potentially different times or time experiences in different directions.
- Degree of focus (the beam-width).
- Depth of engagement (how deeply drawn into the experience a person feels in each direction - this might be a fleeting touch or a full-on blast of emotional memory).

- Whether the client is actually looking in the direction of the gaze (they might be "elsewhere", attention might turn inwards, attention might be split into many directions, and awareness might be in many places at once).
- Degree of movement within a gaze (some are fixed, some wander).
- Any potential internal commentary and emotions, which can be related or might be interference.
- Digital direction jumps or analogue loci.
- Differential awareness and perception between the left and right eyes.
- External phenomena (animals, TV snippets, noises, smells, words, phones, etc).

Between directions there are:

- scanning patterns of the eyes,
- dwell times,
- angular and distance changes,
- shifts in all the parameters of just one direction,
- any repeating or patterns of returning to directions,
- and shifts in body posture.

These ideas for indexing the human experience, related by where the eyes focus, come from the world of radar and electronic surveillance systems. They are great mirrors from the technological world.

In the experience of accessing the wisdom in given directions there is also the wisdom of the angular momentum of the turning to be accessed - a fully parallel reality of insight. There is the wisdom that knows about the directions - the meta-direction wisdom.

Almost anything and everything to do with aiding a fellow human being evolve and emerge can be known simply from working with the subtleties of direction, angle and turning, because the eye focus reveals so much information. The eyes go to where the information is, and so the awareness can then follow. Working with the eyes can lead to efficient ways of resolving the matter being addressed.

The Ark Angle seems to demonstrate, beyond reasonable doubt, the nature of the body-mind interface being the electromagnetic field. With this, the idea that we can un-measure the measurements is also demonstrated.

3.5 Building the Ark Angle

The Ark Angle concept emerged in a "Systems Engineering Meets David Grove" Workshop in July 2005. I had only recently met David, and arranged to bring a group of engineers to explore his work, and to bring in the physics, signal processing and technological neural network knowledge, to explore if we could find some new ways of working with his insight and knowledge.

I was the test subject for his "spinning" process, where I accessed different directions to download information projected into those directions. I immediately asked about other directions than the planar azimuthal directions available from standing and turning. There was no solution, so I suggested a fairground gyroscope.

Two weeks later, we held another group and David had bought one (called a "whirlygig", and now in the possession of Shaun Hotchkiss), which had two rings and a chair in which the client was seated while the machine was moved.

The machine was used experimentally for a few months, and then a third ring was added. Personally, I believed this was too dangerous to manipulate, having nearly having my arm broken while operating it, and that a lighter, portable version was needed.

After Shaun had a major experience in the original machine, he and Caitlin Walker sponsored David in building a new machine. David was not an engineer, and unfortunately he did not listen to my consistent feedback on the mechanical stability, and his attempt had to be binned after a lot of Shaun's and my money had been spent.

I had, meanwhile, suggested an alternative design based upon the flak guns of the Second World War - a rotating base and a pitch-bearing to enable any angle to be found. The main ring was inspired by thinking of hamster wheels and how they can also sit in a kind of "coffee-table" frame. The purpose of this design was to:

- minimise operator health risk by eliminating pinch points created by rings crossing through each other. The two-ring and three-ring versions were inherently dangerous to operate, even at quite slow speeds, and

- enable portability, for transport by car or shipping, by making the Ark Angle capable of quick assembly and dis-assembly .

In 2008, after David's death, and with funding from Charles Wansbrough, I finally found the right designer-mechanic (Charles Dancey) and manufacturing company (Cycles Maximus, engineers: Paul and Dennis) to make a well-engineered machine.

The machine itself weighs in at one hundred and sixty kilos, which is spread over ten main parts. It takes two trained operators about forty minutes to assemble. The optional flooring adds another eighty kilos of wooden trackway that ensures the machine can operate on uneven ground.

The Ark Angle on tour in England, October 2009

The number of rings has been reduced from three to one (roll), making operation safe by removing the scissor action of multiple rings. Two of the rings are replaced by 1) wheels on the legs (yaw) and 2) steering wheels (pitch).

The prototype Ark Angle now resides in Cuernavaca, Mexico, where it is used for Holigral retreats.

The name "Ark Angle" continues the play on words of Holigral (Holy Grail), as the machine works with arcs and angles (Ark, Archangel).

3.6 Summary

Body movement in psycho-active space underlies profound personal change. The different forms of this are based upon turning and moving in space. Combining both enables the pairs of attractors to be undone physically.

The Ark Angle is a potent tool for addressing early years trauma, from conception to toddling.

4 Mind Physics

4.1 Introducing Projection and Sensing

The second level of the pyramid, and the second phase of the cycle is subliminal to most people, but often all-too consciously real for "sensitives" and "autists". This is the realm of projected and received energies, of emotions and trigger-responses. It is also where Physics has its greatest relevance in terms of understanding what is happening.

Many psychologists know that the human perceptual universe is built upon the concept of "projection". Neuro-Linguistic Programming, as defined in the first chapter of the first book on the subject, defines its boundary condition: "everyone is a magician, either consciously or unconsciously wielding magic" and their associated mantra is "perception is projection".

However, I had a broader perspective: the world of "consciousness" beyond the "matrix of magic and magicians", where those who are "conscious" no longer project on/at others; they do not judge, they just accept the world around and themselves as they are. Truly these are the consciously magical people and a very small minority of the human population.

From this perspective, if something is measured (judged, recorded, perceived), then the consciousness is lost into a state of "mind" until such time as that something is un-measured and understood, and "no mind" then re-emerges.

The corollary of this insight is that projection is an emergent consequence of "digital" dissociative events, and as most people have digitally dissociated at some time, they project, albeit unconsciously. Also, as a corollary, where there are attractors there are projections, and where there are projections there are attractors, all formed by the dissociative experiences. The following are all aspects of the projection that emerges from a defining moment.

- Saturday: the entangled relating, between the proton and electron.
- Sunday: the proton attractor within.
- Monday: the electron attractor without (placed on others, objects, situations, etc).
- Tuesday: the mind arising to learn or understand.
- Wednesday: the source of the defining moment (and the self identity emergent from it).
- Thursday: the signals - behaviours and actions.
- Friday: the hindsight: mis-understanding or finally right understanding and resolution.
- The ancestrals are the external actor (father) and the prior self (mother), and the environment around then provides the cultural signal echo to activate in similar contexts.

From this perspective, the whole "normal, projective world matrix" is one of placebo, where the accumulated projective measurements define the relative strength of each placebo, whether physical or mental. This is why the Mormons convert long-dead ancestors, why the first words spoken to a Muslim baby are *"God is great, there is no God but Allah. Muhammad is the messenger of Allah. Come to prayer"*, and also, why and how homeopathy works in life and fails double-blind tests.

Emotions are normally the automatic response to triggers acquired earlier in life. However, if the structures that include these triggers are undone, then emotions are found to be information. They are the projected cues for responsive behaviour when interacting with people who have personal collectives.

The purpose of the model and processes presented in this chapter are to undo the structures, generating a resilient inner peace, awareness and choice of behaviour when interacting with the "mad" social matrix.

4.2 Concepts

How Consciousness "Moves" through a Personal Collective

Awareness moves; the eyes focus in different directions, one can be "lost in thought (or a book/film/story)" or "overcome by feelings". However, so also does the "point of perception" move. For many people this might not be apparent, and for others this is more obviously evident, as they can "remote view" or perceive either associated or dissociated from the body.

The different forms of motion of consciousness are not physically limited, so therefore they more reflect the physics. The motion can be an observable movement; it can be an analogue flow or a digital jump, such as quantum tunnelling (jumping states, like in radioactive decay where an alpha-particle spontaneously appears outside of the nucleus and is accelerated out of the atom); it may be distributed or localised. The physics underlying the motion of consciousness is that of wave packets.

The quantum jumping between selves is "digital" in nature, reflecting the cause, and the gradual or smooth movement is "analogue".

I have seen a "borderline" personality gradually shift over a period of hours from a functional self to a "whingy-baby" self. This was like a gradual, analogue shift between two states of being, but nonetheless the client has no access to "the other state" from either.

One client, with severe ADHD had no connection between her present self and her unconscious or memories, and had several other psychological conditions overlaid. The self was like a ping-pong ball on a stormy sea; bounced around all over the place. By the end of a one-to-one session, all was stable, with suitable barriers in place for her most traumatic memories. She has since lived a functional life, with a job, boyfriend, home and freedom from addictions.

Just by using different names or pronouns or nicknames for a person induces a different self that responds. This quantum-jumps people between selves, but I do not find it useful in creating a smooth, transition of the selves into a oneness.

The smooth movement of self out of the body for astral travelling and remote viewing is, however, not a "jumping" process, and has no dissociative elements pertaining to it.

A natural person will have no automatic jumps of consciousness, but rather, smooth, steady movement. They can "jump" at will, though, but without being forced to do so by the structures.

Sensing

In sensor functions, intrusions that cause dysfunction would comprise either jamming signals or significant threats that are so frequently present that the system is both conditioned and adapted to address that environment, becoming progressively blind to the rest of the world. Mostly, the purpose of jamming is to deny awareness of threats.

The other problems in sensor functions are "clutter", which are signals of no present interest, or noise that looks like signals, and "noise", which is the environmental background, and which can also interfere with the process of discriminating signals. It is a much simpler environment to grow up in the desert as opposed to a large city.

The result of a person or group having sensing dysfunction would be to misclassify many normal events as threats. In other words, the system is biased towards perceiving threats, due to over-training on a limited sample of stimulation.

From Bayesian decision theory, the false-alarm rate has to be high because the consequences of making a false-safe decision could be life-threatening, so the system biases towards errors classifying more signals as threats[46]. We can see this in the people and countries with the most weapons; their fear is primal.

If the system is developed initially in a high-threat environment, it biases its sense of the world towards perceiving threats. In other scenarios later in its life the system will still bias itself towards deciding something is a threat, because the system believes the probability of threat is high to start with. Because threats are, by their nature, potentially damaging to the owners of the intelligence system, they occupy a significant amount of processing. In a system with limited resources this means that there is correspondingly less resource available for more general learning and development. For example,

---

[46] The mathematics of mininum-risk decision making is as follows, given an input, x, the probability of x being a threat (A), $P(A \mid x)$ is: $P(A \mid x) = P(A).P(x \mid A) / P(x)$, where $P(x) = P(A).P(x \mid A) + P(not-A).P(x \mid not-A)$, A is threat, "$not-A$" is "not threat", and $P(A)$ is the prior probability of A.

it might be too dangerous to focus on one thing so completely that another, potentially dangerous, signal could be completely ignored.

Awareness Cycle

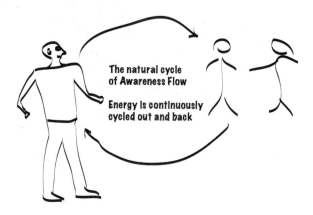

Awareness cycle: above

Human measurements are created mainly through "defining moments" where a person changes, mostly through a mini shock or trauma, after which they become cold - it is common wisdom that people in shock or who have had accidents need to be kept warm, given warm drinks, and so on. In this moment, a pair of attractors is created: an internal emotional responder (proton; inside the body) and an external trigger (electron; outside the body).

The cold happens because new energy has to go into projecting and sensing the world, as the old projecting energy is now encapsulated in the attractors. Thereafter when the present moment reflects the geometry of the defining moment, the trigger activates the responder.

During the normal flow of events, the projecting-sensing cycle continues uninterrupted. Awareness is equal in all directions, like a sphere expanding out from a point, until something happens to train focus, after which the focus of attention structure is like a useful early-in-life measurement.

Human Sensor-System Measurement (Shock)

This kind of human measurement is made through the focus and movement of awareness, which is interrupted or recorded through experiences like "shock", "association", "intrusion" and "non-understanding". Thus, a person records an experience until it is understood, or until life force disconnected by a shock is reconnected, or until life force associated into something external is recovered through reconnection, or until the intruded life force is reconnected and returned to its source (whence it came).

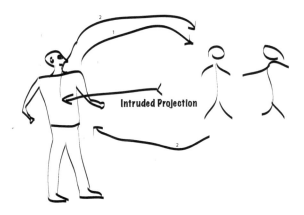

Defining moment: above

This is called a **defining moment.** Some of the cycling energy in the time-space location of the field of focus at the time (see diagram below) is converted to a new potential energy[47] of the structure-measurement of the defining moment. That means new life force is required to be output to continue the projecting-sensing, and so thermal energy is converted into the kinetic energy of the sensing-projecting.

As a result of a measurement, an aspect of mind comes into being; each aspect of mind reflects a defining moment. The aspect might be a curiosity into a subject, or a thought pattern or a voice or a gesture or feeling. As they are un-measured, so does this aspect of mind cease, and without measurements, there is "no mind", naturally.

---

[47] Potential Energy is the Physics term for energy stored in a structure, like the water in a dam.

Part of the potential energy has gone into the form of attractors that enable access to the defining moment. These attractors will create triggers, which are signals for recovering the energy lost into the structure. These structures and attractors can be useful or problematic. As far as human healing is concerned, only the problematic structures require undoing.

The person's system will subsequently keep attracting people and situations that re-enact the defining moment, in order to recover the life force; albeit unwittingly on the part of the present consciousness. As a result a whole series of events can overlay a single, potentially fairly innocuous event, making an attractor stronger and stronger. If it becomes all-consuming then the literal equivalent of a black hole is formed, and an obsession becomes the entire focus of a person's life.

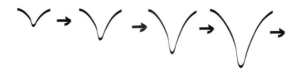

Overlaid defining moments create deeper attractors

A defining epoch is like an extended moment, perhaps even a whole lifetime, where an environmental condition is so present that it is absorbed, like osmosis, into the self, and becomes a conditioning factor, albeit highly unconscious; like living in an only-English-speaking culture for example.

Projection is defined as the act, consciously or unconsciously, of placing an "electron" attractor at/on/over another person or object or concept.

Signals are defined as the attempt of the dissociated aspects to be noticed, and thus recovered. This is why it is so important to accept every aspect of the client. Just like a child plays "hide and seek", and if not found, gives off tell-tale signs, gradually these signals become louder and LOUDER. Drugs may suppress something for a while but eventually the signals will overcome anything blocking them.

Measurement as a "waveform collapse"

All possibilities exist until something is measured, and in the measuring it is transformed and fixed; until such time as an un-measuring happens.

This idea comes from the basic quantum physics so well explained by Richard Feynman in his "Lectures on Physics, Part III", where he describes how something (and everything) is both a particle and a wave, existing as a probability field in all space and time until it is measured; either in location or momentum accurately, or both inaccurately. This wave-particle exists not only in real space-time but also in imaginary space-time.

The theory of physics, used to explain phenomena from the particle scale up to the cosmic scale, uses both real and imaginary space-time. The implication is that our scale of reality is also both real and imaginary.

Measurement fixes something into the "real" using an expectation operator[48] that integrates the product of the measurement space with the wave-function probability field[49] of what is being measured. A measured object is the collapsed result in space-time. In this case, the real becomes the neurological pattern and response, and the imaginary is the locations of the human attractor pair of proton and electron.

When the observer measures, the probabilistic energy field loses some energy that is collapsed into a structure that holds the measurement. The human observer experiences this as the cold after a shock. Un-measuring a shock leads to the opposite experience, a marked heating, and the probabilistic energy field re-expands. The neurology will no longer trigger; this is physical proof.

---

[48] An expectation operator is a piece of mathematics used, for example, in quantum physics to integrate over all space and time to find a location or momentum, depending on what is being measured. As the cosmic-joke nature of its name says, "expectation"; it measures what is expected.

[49] A wave function probability field is how something is representing until it is measured, in quantum physics.

Fractal

Further to the idea of defining moments is the corollary that there are many, and so the selves become nested into an internal family tree of defining moments, ultimately creating the presently-perceived self or selves.

Each measurement results in a fragmentation of the consciousness of the self of before the measurement, into one or more products of the measurement. After many years of measurements a person is absolutely not an individual but rather a personal collective, where each individual aspect represents a measurement - a piece of mind requiring to understand or resolve or clear a measurement.

As a space-time measurement happens, it appears to be recorded holographically as a focus of attention plus its context and indexing coding. It makes sense that the self of before a measurement records it, and that the self after the measurement has to deal with the consequences thereof.

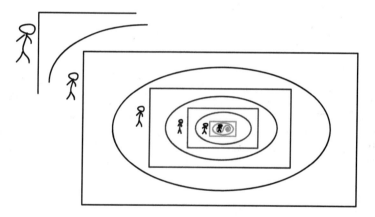

The fractal self

It is rather like each self is the mother/God of the next self, and the projective world around of the measurement is the father.

Consider a set of Russian dolls, where the creator is around the created. The innermost, smallest self is the present one. The primal projection, therefore, for a human being is the ancestral coded DNA of the parents, influenced by the environment at the moment of conception.

A person becomes like a whole family tree, and a whole series of incidents can overlay an early attractor. Rather like how an atom interacts chemically with its environment, so the human being's array of electron and proton attractors connects with people through their life who have appropriate responding attractors of their own. This is the person, held within the matrix.

Outside of the matrix are people who are like the Noble gases, inert and non-reacting. The most powerfully attracting people tend to have only one major attractor - just like the atomic elements with one spare electron or one missing electron; they pull other people into their orbits.

However, these people are also just as enmeshed in the matrix as you, even though they sense the projective energy level and probably believe they are "masters" - actually "master hypnotists" would fit. You can tell

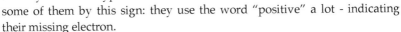

some of them by this sign: they use the word "positive" a lot - indicating their missing electron.

If something happens, but all flows and is understood, then no measurement happens and the person stays fully embodied. However, this is a rarity, likely only in families of conscious people (e.g. travellers or Tibetans or some few Holigral graduates), or other people, who might have used, for example, marijuana to attain awakened consciousness. Holigral makes these obsolete, and pointless as the consciousness is natural.

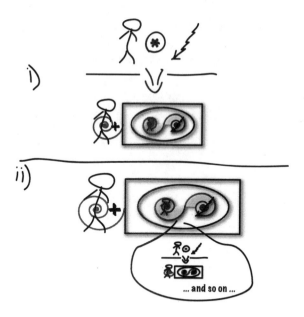

Another perspective of the family-tree of self-creation

The family tree is shown in the diagram above, from another perspective; of the parents of each new set of self-children. The mother is the previous self and the father is the intruded projection; just like egg and sperm.

4.3 "Sunday" Processes

The first process, called "Re-Scaling", addresses any scale of problem, including one's whole life, if one really wants the consequences. It is a gradual process taking days to eventually coincide the creator self with the present self.

The other two processes, "Pronoun Scaling" and the "Truth Process", were born from the realisation I experienced after had escaped from the projective matrix in October 2006. They basically exploit the power of the "right understanding" combined with embodying the perspective of the creator of the situation - a previous self or indeed a long-passed ancestor or being.

The pronoun scaling works with chains of projections, following the chain of causation, even to "God" and beyond to the greater self around that concept. It works with victim, persecutor, witness or rescuer trauma.

The truth work is like keyhole surgery compared with the open-heart of re-scaling. It will deconstruct an entire tree of beliefs, and then enable a sound reconstruction of something more useful. It also goes back to God or beyond, and can include getting "the cosmic joke".

4.4 Re-Scaling

As I progressed, in early 2006, I started to move away from strictly spatial and geometric forms, and found naturally emergent ways of enabling emergence to happen[50]. One of these, David Grove called "loading B", because more and more information was requested about the subject (B) at the beginning of a session, and then the space became psychoactive naturally, without manipulating geometry[51].

When I told him about this, David described the phenomenon as "the tails wags the dog", because B was leading A's movements and space [A is the client]. Literally the body language and focus of the person was related to the paper on which the drawing and writing was placed. The next logical

---

[50]The development of any subject will always go through a phase of being referred from another perspective. Once it is fully developed it becomes self-referential. The "C" programming language was first compiled in FORTRAN before it could be re-compiled in "C" by its prototype FORTRAN-based compiler. Later versions could be fully self-referential. The same was true for Grovian Metaphor Therapy, Clean Space, and became true for emergence as it shed its roots of space and hypnotic delivery.

[51]Manipulating Geometry was the initial way to engage a person into the precise neurological index for a change process; otherwise the wrong thing might get affected, with unwelcome side-effects. As we moved away from roots based in spatial thinking, we could achieve the same results with less contrivance on the part of the facilitator; in other words, we could facilitate more cleanly.

While some Fortran programmers preferred to stay with Fortran, most moved to "C". The same is true for the use of Emergence; only those associated into the old ways would stick with them, but the Geometric Start and patterns labelling spaces are relatively inefficient and will linger as long as the attachments to them.

step was to find out if this process could then continue under its own momentum.

I brought in the idea from fluid mechanics that all the information is actually on the boundary. The boundaries and boundary conditions are where to focus attention; just like the boundary of a black hole is its event horizon, and the turbulence in a stream is driven by the small irregularities of its boundaries.

David resonated with this idea, as he was always interested in being able to find a boundary for a client's perceptual world which, once formed, would allow a phase of development and change to happen within a controlled context.

From this we developed a new process, that we called "scaling" at the time. This gradually explored the space around an initial loading of B, until a first boundary was defined. By having faith with this algorithm and learning not to resort to manipulating the geometry we had hit gold; a consistent and reliable universal process for undoing cosmological boundaries[52] that required mainly patience and acceptance from the facilitator - the process could be a highly frustrating experience for the client, and being the guinea-pig, I can vouch for this.

As a result of this development we could, for the first time in the lifetime of clean facilitation, go through many cosmological boundaries. We could reconnect many dissociated aspects, and were able to deal with large numbers of pronouns and whole subjects, like "fear". The consequences on me were profound, and my personal intuition and insight grew far beyond my previous beliefs.

Connections started to form to ancient traditions; how and why they worked, why they were less efficient for modern occidentals; and my sense of the world was frequently reborn.

---

[52] The cosmological boundary is that between the present self and the creating previous self. It is like the sound barrier or the speed of light; one cannot travel back and forth between them; there is no memory of the moment before, only a shadow of that which was.

Starting Conditions for Re-Scaling

A client enters your room with a "presenting issue" with an interpretation that makes logical sense to their adult rational mind, and a belief system that supports and sustains their reality. The really useful information they give will not be in the interpreted, conscious words, but in asides, literal listening and mishearing of the words, gestures, tics, drawing, writing and sounds like coughs, ums and errs. Why?

The very first thing they say is probably the most important verbal communication. Why?

The job of a system is to preserve its present structure. In particular, the dominant consciousness of a person very likely fears the outcome of change that results in a change of topology – it fears "losing control", suffering as it does from the illusion of control. Therefore, whatever work is undertaken has to either keep this conscious mind busy and engaged while change happens, or work within its control paradigm.

The person is a collective consciousness, with the "normal" dominant consciousness mostly located in a tiny volume in or near the head - say one cubic millimetre, but probably more like one cubic micron[53]. The different parts of consciousness each communicate however they can around the constraints of getting around the filters of the conscious mind.

For example, when the client writes answers to questions, each answer can be in the same or different handwriting. Each handwriting style represents a different consciousness at a different age and location. Each drawing a client does shows both an age and reveals the relevant body parts. By having a collection of drawings from children of different ages, you can learn to calibrate the age. Similarly, by learning the ages of handwriting, you can calibrate its age, too.

This process can be run for a few minutes or for days depending upon the scale of the subject being addressed. Typically it might take a few days for a whole life, and a few minutes for a business issue.

---

[53] The scale of the self reflects the out-of-scale-ness of the starting conditions, and can be measured by the ratios of the six re-scaled drawings to the real scale of the finishing conditions.

Questions / Instructions	Comments
Represent your starting statement.	{Here the starting is very broad, but then it becomes totally oriented to working on paper.}
(Write or draw or both or sculpt something or dance it.)	
"What else goes on there?"	Keep adding more about the starting statement.
Keep adding more and more.	Occasionally step back and notice what new insights might be emerging.
What else do I know about this?	
What else does [...] know about this?	
What goes around the edges / sides / above / below?	As and when needed, step back and notice if any shape or form or pattern emerges. Keep adding more and more, around and around.
So re-draw or re-scale what you now see.	As before, keep adding more and more, until another new pattern emerges. This might happen 6 or 7 times before the process completes.
And what goes around that?	
And what else?	

"The proof of the pudding is in the eating."

Re-Scaling Transcript

On the right, is the first "drawing", made by the client.

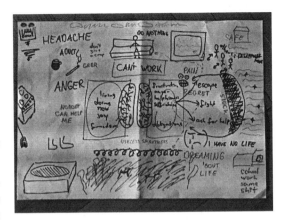

The elements in this will appear re-structured into their correct form in the last drawing; the frame of the defining moment.

The next three drawings show the gradual process of the client moving their awareness from the central focus of this piece of paper to the context around.

Extending the drawing, just starting the process of finding wider contexts

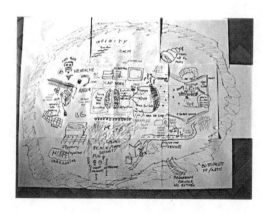

A first boundary is drawn - with an "exit" in the bottom right hand corner

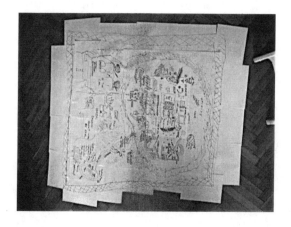

A second boundary layer (wall-fence)

After this "bounding", we can now see the beginning of two patterns: a rounded, inner boundary, and a rectangular outer boundary. The drawing below is where the client has redrawn the above - into the rectangular "fence" structure at the centre-left of the drawing below.

The FIRST re-scale

The following five drawings are again all gradual widening of perspective around the focus of the starting re-scaling above.

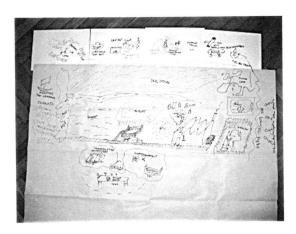

Extending this first re-scaling

Further extending the first re-scaling

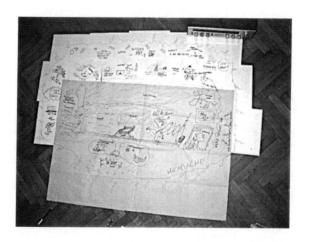

Even further extending the first re-scaling

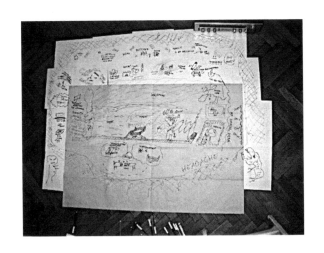

Continuing to extend

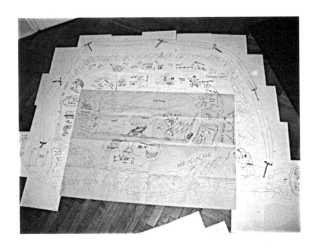

Running out of floor space for this first re-scale; the second beckons

Zooms of the bottom left (right :-)) and bottom right corners (left :-))

Only when the limits of the room are met does the client choose to re-scale - next drawing.

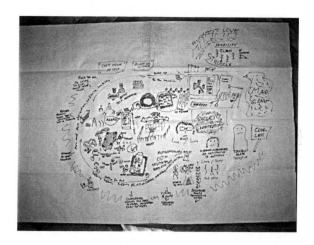

The SECOND e-scale

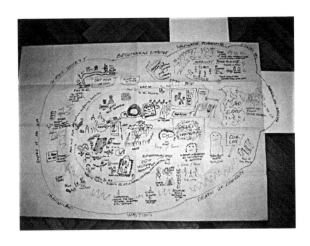

Extending the second re-scale

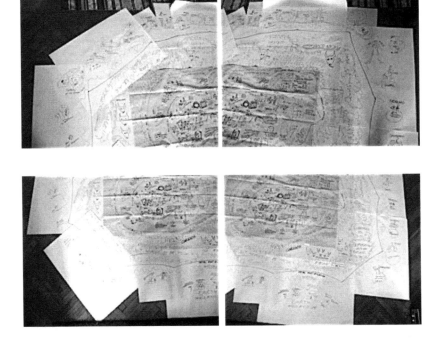

a little more!

The THIRD re-scale

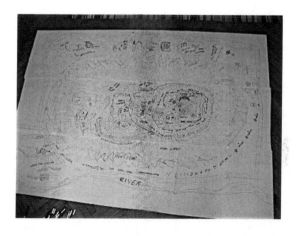

End of third re-scale: notice how this could be foetal

The fourth re-scale will often, probably normally, have a different topology as the client starts to transition into the territory of the previous self from the defining moment.

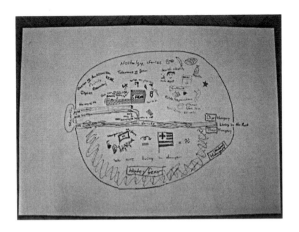

4th re-scale

Extending the 4th re-scale

At the fifth re-scale the topology of the end is becoming revealed; the territory of the mother and birthing.

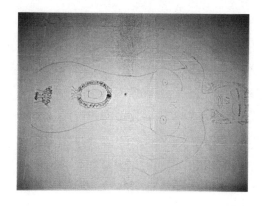

The 5th Re-scale

Extending the 5th Re-scale

The sixth re-scale is linguistic, as the signals flow to complete their jobs.

> Client: And mum feels it's crap that she had to compromise with this man :D, It's circa above the table, Mum is a bit too big for this perspective, But the furniture is more or less right as you said, two close perspectives
>
> *Fac: maybe 2 dissociated bits?*

Client: I think the other one was father's, right after he came :), At least I felt a strong connection when I stepped into that one, and that nervous-uncertain thing is gone

Fac: makes sense

Client: So now I have to find the space for the lamp, right? I have a "let's get this over with" feeling :D

Fac: around the whole thing to rescale towards the time before you were dissociated, I'm afraid

Client: How? What else can be around this one?

Fac: right

Client: I just see the physical world around it

Fac: good, keep drawing that ...The house, their car etc keep going

Client: The lake, the town, The country, Europe, globe

Fac: around

Client: Galaxy, Universe

Fac: Around

Client: Here & now feeling somewhere in my heart   [the body is touched, finally!]

The 6th re-scale has happened in the mind-questions-answers. Then, it is about moving forward the reconnected body (in time; to now).   The questions go left-right-left-right by feet, so right-left-right-left by brain hemisphere.

Re-Scaling Transcript Analysis

Patience is needed; serious patience, as this process takes days, and everything has to be reflected back onto the paper, including meta-comments and asides and conversational interludes.

The pictures show a gradual shifting of perspective, with certain boundary themes recurring, reflecting the layering of structures upon the attractors of the primal dissociation while in the womb, leading to their client's birthing process. The ancestral energies are clear to see in the drawings relating to concentration camps, and the group unconscious aspects emerge in the depiction of monsters around the edges.

Even though this analysis reveals some of the nature of the process, it remains impossible to cheat, as the congruence required at every level and stage will be broken, and the facilitators are wise to such things, having seen enough attempts. There are people who try to control appearances, their words, their drawings and communications, and "fake it to make it"; they will only cheat themselves and remain dissociated if they try such measures. As it is.

The key understanding to acquire from this transcript relates to the moment when the dissociated self touches the body of the present self; literally the experience is of the person looking out of the eyes of their younger self - looking from the body. The situation is that the younger self is now scaled to the present body and focus of awareness. Therefore the measurement is unmeasured by the alignment of the consciousness into the exact geometry of the moment of measurement.

The re-associated fragment of self then grows up to the present age, in an accelerated life-review kind of experience. The present self can find this a little disconcerting to re-experience what may be childlike or adolescent emotions and reactions. But, if they are not judged (re-measured) and are instead allowed to complete their purpose then everything stabilises into a new, more present self.

When enough of these experiences of re-associating have happened, a critical mass effect occurs, and the present self expands to the body boundary, and beyond, unto the limits of the universe and back, to a one to one scale. The person is "at one", living at one-to-one scale with the world around, with a healthy sense of proportion. And the results are permanent; they do not relapse.

There is nothing really to compare to this experience; it is like living bliss and also being fully functional in the world. No doubt the resultant brain waves will show the same kind of signals as the Tibetan monks who have spent a lifetime maintaining beingness. This is as it is. It is possible to live a normal life AND have the benefits of the awakened self, to live without suffering, while still enjoying the rollercoaster. It is called "having your cake and eating it".

There is an old saying *"The one-eyed man is king in the land of the blind."* This was said by a sighted person. In a real land of the blind they would not believe the sighted person. This is called the "Cassandra Effect", after the Trojan priestess whose predictions were never believed by the Trojans.

Instead, the blind people would value the most acute hearing, the best sense of touch and smell and taste. People with such paranormal skills disguise them as mind tricks and "cold reading" in order to allay the fears of the otherwise paranoid audience.

Holigral is like Cassandra. What can gained is beyond the belief of the normal person. It was beyond my own beliefs before I stumbled across what is now known.

In a 2D world, such as a table-top, a being that exists in that world perceives the fingers on the table to be separate entities. So a flock is seen as a set of individuals working in local relation rather than an emergent group mind.

Only the 3D perspective gives the insight that the fingers are part of something greater than they can sense.

The end point of facilitation, from the facilitator's perspective, is when a client has become "at one with" the starting conditions; "seeing things as they are". In other words, they no longer have an issue, or problem, or goal or outcome; they are just getting on with life and it is happening. This is called being in "one to one" scale with the world. It is also the condition for enlightenment, or perhaps as it is better entitled, "embodiment".

4.5 Truth Work

"It's always someone else's fault."

The chain of Cause and Effect in ancestral belief systems

Mostly, our actions are actually reactions, using behaviours and words that we learned so long ago that we cannot even consciously remember when they came to us. Our beliefs follow a similar pattern, except that as we grow we may take on and discard a whole series of beliefs, both superficial and fundamental. We may choose to adopt something new, or it may fit so well with our existing structure that it just slips into place unnoticed.

From the Buddhist idea of "Right Understanding", combined with the realisation that healing comes from looking through the embodied eyes of the self of before the traumatic defining moment, what if one could get there directly, using the logic of cause and effect? This question led to the process as described, but going further, down the entire chain of projections until before its very beginning, thus freeing also the ancestrally-inherited traumas.

It can be difficult, if not impossible, to work out why something has happened, from the current viewpoint. Too much has been obscured by layers of more recent events and their consequences, and the rationalisations and justifications that we create in order to make sense of them.

The truth process is a simple, profound and highly effective way of getting to the root cause of something that we don't understand. It is a recursive process, in which the direction of the next question is solely based on the answer given to the previous one. This way, you can navigate gently through all the layers that time and your experiences have created, until you eventually arrive at the point where you really comprehend how it came to be.

Many personal development methods require that you   take full responsibility for everything that happens to you. Holigral processes allow for the possibility that other peoples' actions and words have had an impact on you. After all, the only way that we have learned everything in our lives is through other people. All our words, all our behaviours, all our reactions have their origins in other people.

Every belief or perception a person has about themselves or the world has come from a series of cause-effect events that goes into their personal past, and very probably into ancestral and cultural roots. By navigating the chain of cause-effect, a person arrives at an understanding of its fundamental nature and the belief is released. Then, a new "tree of belief" can be formed.

We use a wording associated with truth and blame - not blame in a negative sense, but in the sense of cause, because each blamed person then blames the next, and so on, as the whole belief systems and emotional associations are deconstructed.

This work is more like keyhole surgery, compared to the open heart surgery of the Rescaling process. It is useful for addressing pinpoint issues.

The Cosmic Joke is revealed ...

Questions / Instructions	**Comments**
Write down your opening statement or belief.	Or speak, or draw, or represent this.
What had to be true, in order, for this to have become true?	
What had to be true for that to have become true?	Repeat until "someone else" is mentioned.

What had to be true in order for them to have become like that?	and repeat for the next person, etc, until "society" or a more general belief emerges like, "that's just how it was".
[continue for this person as for the client.]	
What had to be true on order for it to have become like that?	Asking about the cultural or cosmological cause ...
	until it is "the universe" or "God" who is to blame.
"So, it's all his/its/their fault, then."	God is big enough to take the blame. This is often associated with a release of laughter.
And now what can be true?	Repeat until repeats are no longer needed.

This process does not require a full downloading at the start, unlike many of the others. It can begin with a simple statement, and needs no other preparation. A transcript is below, showing how it works in practice.

[Start of transcript.]

1 What had to be true in order for you to have become the way you are now?

[Stunned look.] My first thought was "that's an evil question", and the obvious answer which sounds a bit trite is, "everything that's happened to me so far".

2 What has to be true in order for this to have been true?

Umm, all my, everything that's happened to me has had an effect somewhere along the line, I can't discount anything.

3 What has to be true in order for this to have been true?

[Sits right back in the chair. More of a grimace than a smile.] Hm. Back to the question, [scratches head, hand in front of mouth] every event impacts me because it adds to my store of experience and therefore everything else has to accommodate it and I can't discount anything because if its happened then its happened, its like the saying you cannot un-invent something. I do this a lot, don't I, my answers have two streams.

4 What has to be true in order for this to have been true?

[Smile.] Well now I've got three sets of answers to follow have I? [Smiles.] The obvious answer is because I'm a detailer and I cannot leave any avenue unexplored.

5 What has to be true in order for this to have been true?

Because its like female shopping, I want to get all the information I possibly can before making a decision. [for the reader -this is a female answering.]

6 And what has to be true in order for this to have been true?

Because I've made a punt based on intuition or too little information and its been wrong.

7 And what had to be true in order for this to have been true?

I think the problem was not so much me getting things wrong but the reactions of people around me to me getting them wrong.

8 What had to be true in order for them to have those reactions? [The SWITCH question.]

And I don't know if even they did, that's just how I remember it, but assuming that they did, it was probably because of their expectations that they placed on me that I was the incredibly intelligent little daughter. That's a really hard one to live up to especially when you are small because there is no scope for trial and error and getting things wrong. and what I don't know is how much was pressure from them and how much was pressure I put on myself.

9 What has to be true in order for a person to put pressure on another person?

Because they want that other person to conform to their expectations, to the image that's been built around them.

10 And what had to be true in order for this to have become true, for them?

Well it might be that they are using that other person to look better. Or might be that they want other people to believe them all the time and if that other person lets them down in any way then its like they have not been telling the truth about them, so it implies their judgement is flawed.

11 And what had to be true in order for this to have become true, for them?

I think that they want to appear grown up and responsible and trustworthy.

12 And what had to be true in order for this to have become true, for them?

Because they've done some things which were monumentally not grown up and responsible and trustworthy in their eyes and were living the consequences every day.

13 And what had to be true in order for this to have become true, for them?

I think there was a dose of cultural and social pressure mixed with a little ignorance.

14 And what had to be true in order for this to have become true?

They wanted to be part of something that was happening all around them.

15 And what had to be true in order for this to have become true?

It was exciting.

So what do you know now?

That they beat themselves up for years for a momentary lapse of common sense. People around them took the consequences.

16 And what had to be true in order for this to have become true, for them?

Because it caused a life change for them in a direction that they did not intend and because they had not chosen it they resisted and resented.

17 And what had to be true in order for this to have become true, for them?

They were too stuck with their attachment to what they had wanted rather than accepting what they had got.

18 And what had to be true in order for them to have become like that?

Well I think it was because they had grown up in quite a repressive society they had had a glimpse of something different and had it snatched away almost as quickly as they had seen it. So I think they felt they had done themselves out of being part of something that was very exciting at the time.

19 And what had to be true in order for this to have become true?

Well then they permanently shackled themselves with commitments and responsibilities at a time when popular culture involved living free of them.

20 And what had to be true in order for this to have become true, for them?

I suppose they made a choice. They didn't have to make the choice they did at the time, there were other options available.

21 And what had to be true in order for that to have been true?

I don't think they could countenance doing anything other than what they did. I also think that it wasn't what either of them intended or wanted at the time.

So what do you know now?

That a lot of their behaviour that I didn't understand when I was younger was them lashing out at anyone and everything against the situation that they had put themselves into. It was a childish rant I suppose just on a grand scale.

1 So now what can be true for you?

Well I don't have to take their actions from the past quite so personally any more.

2 So now what can be true for you?

That feels like role reversal, I feel like the indulgent parent dealing with a little kid having a tantrum.

3 So now what can be true for you?

Perversely given the last answer, feels like um I can just have a completely adult relationship with them, without all that childish stuff getting in the way.

4 So now what can be true for you?

I don't know, I'm just happy with that. I've tackled this from a lot
of angles, and I've never quite made that progress on it before.

[End of transcript.]

The process released a structure the client had inherited from their parents.

4.6 Pronoun Scaling

This process emerged from putting together the ideas of the Truth Process,
Re-Scaling and the model of their being six steps between different aspects of
self. The idea is to undo a chain of projective intrusions or extrusions by
following the daisy-chain of the pronouns. It is like a "join the dots" puzzle,
where the pronouns are the dots, beginning with the body and ending "me,
here and now".

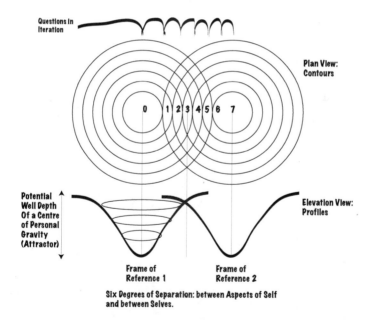

*The patterns of six questions navigate across the boundary layers between pronouns,
by choosing a consistent direction of inside or around.*

There are four conditions that we seek to alleviate to bring personal wholeness, namely:

- Removal of foreign objects (that which has come from outside and embedded into the person) – separating the foreign object from the client (incoming projections);
- Recovery of self embedded into the environment (metaphysical, physical objects and people) – de-fragmenting the structure;
- Recovery of imploded self – expanding out a black hole (i.e. bringing mind back to body);
- Undoing one's own projections onto others;

All these require addressing from the perspectives of victim, persecutor, rescuer and witness.

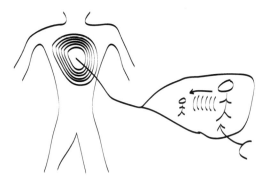

Pronoun triggers are layered under the sequences of incoming emotional radiations

The journey through pronouns has to serve all four conditions, and sometimes all four may occur within the same journey. All journeys start and end with the self that is "here and now", and involve changing scale inside or outside – the initial communication will be from the "end-client".

Emotional systems come in layers; the first layer is the last one that was intruded, and the deepest layer is the first one intruded. After having found the pronoun, the emotions ought to now be outside of the pronoun, and therefore suitable for tracing down ancestral or other projective sequences.

Starting from the opening communication, there is a choice: to scale IN or OUT. As a rule, it is most economical to go INSIDE something within the body and to go OUTSIDE (around) of something outside of the body. But, this rule is arbitrary and subject to the precise local conditions - in other words to your intuition and subtle differences like "feeling angry" versus "feeling anger" - the former is INSIDE; the latter is OUTSIDE the body.

Starting from going around, a pronoun will emerge, and the normal rule is to establish age and clothing (the "wearing" questions in the table below) and what is around that pronoun. After the first "around" question it is worth asking "And is there anything else?"

If the statement owns a feeling then go INSIDE the pronoun's body. If there is a feeling outside, it belongs to another person/being, so next, find out who is there. Follow that and go INSIDE that person.

This is done because this will now permanently separate the bad feeling from the client (you might be the client if you are facilitating yourself), and re-associate it back to its source within the other person. You then follow this back to another person or until its power has completely faded or even been replaced by something useful and strong, or return to a pronoun of the client.

Questions	Comments
"And whereabouts could [that] be, in your body, head or outside?"	In response to a "feeling" statement.
"And what could be inside that?" (six times)	
"How old could that [pronoun] be?"	Locating the real-world environment of the next pronoun.
"What could [age] be wearing?	

"And who or what could be there?"

"And whereabouts could [emotion] be coming from in their body, their head or from outside?"

The trail of projections go from one person to another, often down chains of ancestors.

"An what could be inside [that location]?" (six times)

Continue to go inside six times, and you get to the inner-child pronoun of the other person.

Continue with the above two steps: "age, wearing, who else, where in their body, inside" six times...

Continue until, paradoxically, the journey ends back with "me here and now", or far enough down a chain as to be no concern. Even pronouns like "God" are treated the same.

With the pronouns which have no age, they need exploring contextually - possibly metaphorically, possibly finding a size/shape/form and then scaling around or **inside** that, possibly "inging" an ageless, timeless pronoun.

Pronoun Scaling Transcript

The following is an *e-chat transcript* of advanced pronoun scaling (primarily). Grammar and spelling have been left as typed.

The facilitator is leading the client from pronoun to another person or cause, and then goes inside that person to their inner child, and so on. This is following a chain of incoming projections back to their source. It gradually decouples the person from the "starting problem" until it is no longer their problem.

[Start of transcript.]

> Client: can I ramble to you?
> *Fac: Aye.*

Client: Ta. I'm noticing the perfection very regularly. the gap between crappy mind, and ever present now-ness is certainly closing my creations are creating me. my integrity has gone through the roof. Comparatively i have some very close, mazing friends and the love is changing everything. so is the honesty but, in terms of getting workshops n stuff together.. and really feeling to make life progress and $$$ its still challenging

Fac: aye

Client: i feel that iv not gone without the appropriate navigations.. but i still want to work with [name].. and he's so hard to get ahold of- even when he's not, feel like i shouldn't contact people if there busy

Fac: how old the "I" saying "should" ... pronoun-scale

Client: yeah.. 12

Fac: wearing ... who's there etc

Client: and ok- i spose i realise i don't need any other coaching.. im so good at doing it myself, now.., but-ok:, red cap.. dad is there, dads tired and pained

Fac: where is the should coming from inside his tired and pained

Client: aand busy.. n tells me he doesn't have time, hmm.. his head and arm and back and everything

Fac: inside that should inside there?

Client: love..

Fac: inside ...

Client: of work, and support.. and well, himself- doing the best he can

Fac: inside that

Client: just a bit more tiredness...

Fac: inside ...

Client: and even loneliness at having to do it all himself. (LOL)

Fac: inside ...

Client: courage.. endless strength and fortitude, godliness.. of manhood father soul

Fac: inside

Client: God

Fac: inside

Client: perfection..soul serivce.. patterns upon patterns on patterns

Fac: inside

Client: endless causes and conditions

Fac: inside

Client: to which we can transcend

Fac: how old is the "we"?

Client: hmm..4

Fac: wearing ...who's there

Client: blue..mum and grandma and assorted family

Fac: and what's inside them?

Client: all different kinds of stuff, busy-ness, distraction

Fac: inside busyness

Client: non-presentness

Fac: inside

Client: obligation.. responsiblitiy

to me

Fac: how old

Client: to family.. and burdens of bullshit

1- b'day. hmm... no, 9months.. since conception, me crying and screaming

Fac: around ...

Client: doctors.. nurses , dad, the bloody dopy pain of the epidural , no pain.. nothing gained

Fac: where does that come from?   [Asked because this IS the SOURCE client.]

Client: no conscious connection to mum.. wamr embrace of d dad , which bit

Fac: where does that come from

Client: it allcomes from me- aYe. god

Fac: where does that come from

114

Client: u, everyone- everything. me. here. now

Fac: ok

Client: the navigations are getting so bloody easy and quick

Fac: aye, they do, quicker n easier

Client: until?

Fac: nothing to process

Client: total oblivion with choice, and universe and mastery?

Fac: aye

Client: HAHAHAHAHAHAHAHAHa ahh   ahhhh. (ahem) hmph ok. Thankyou. THANKYOU.

[END OF TRANSCRIPT]

The pattern meandered through six pronouns, internal or external, before landing back "here and now". The client was freed of the "should not contact people if they're busy". Even if the pronoun is "God", the process continues, treating all pronouns equally.

Also note that cultural pronouns are also just more pronouns ('they", "people", "others", "someone", "no-one", "anybody", "[the] culture", "society", "the establishment", etc).

4.7 Conclusion of the Sunday Phase

While these energies are normally subliminal, the gradual clearing of automatic responses enables the real environment to be sensed emotionally and energetically. Literally, one can learn to taste or to smell a room or people, from their fields, and to know the same kind of knowing that the animals have of people.

There is a danger that clients prefer to address all their "victim" aspects, and do not face the harm they have caused, intentionally or accidentally, through their own projections. Because of this, the Monday processes were invented - next.

5 Measurement

5.1 The Measurement Function

The next level of the pyramid is reflection and measurement, which is the Monday phase of the cycle.

The measurement system inherits the distortions of the sensor system and the consequences. It hold the attractors, and also matches the energy received from the environment against the strongest attractors as a kind of early-warning system - they trigger in response to "threats" [predators] or "opportunities" [prey]. The primal system is always on alert for situations that resemble the conditions that created the attractors, which is part of the system's desire to learn from the experience and thus escape a re-experience.

If one considers how an unsupervised, self-organising, neural network learns, by gradually creating groupings of similarity and structures to recognise differences, then the centres of gravity of the classes of recognised objects, like words, reflect the learning conditions of each object (word). The earliest learned symbols have primacy in such networks. Thus both the neural network and the brain's connectivity reflect the order and strength of programming.

In both kinds of networks, under-training leads to a lack of discrimination, and over-training leads to wrong classification of events and inabilities to generalise outside of the trained areas of recognition - "like a fish out of water".

As a simple example, once trained in English as a first language on its own, it is difficult to hear the different sound patterns and discriminate oriental languages, whereas children raised bi-lingually take longer to learn but have an inherently greater ability to acquire more languages later in life.

The following diagram shows different views on how we can interpret signals and choose interventions by considering the fractal nature of the model. The consequence of this model is that, using only ten questions, in principle one can accurately and uniquely profile an individual human being, diagnose their situation, and determine what can happen next.

What I call "human signals intelligence" is the art of reading the signals being shown by a client, a business, a state, a culture, a religion, a team, or the world around.

This model is capable of fractal expansion, as shown on the cylinder below. The kinds of information that we can use includes job, car, house, family, clothing, postures, gestures, turns of phrase, nonverbal sounds, house contents, office layout, driving style, hobbies or sports, entertainment preferences; literally anything to do with you.

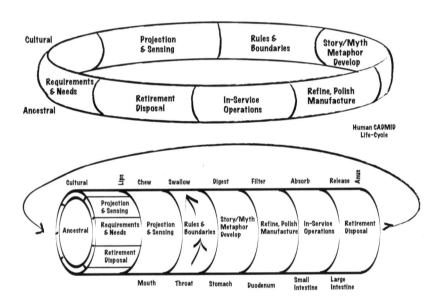

Wheels within wheels; the fractal

Human Measurement 3 - Coding

The human measurements are mostly coded in space-time-metaphor. However the more subtle fields of cultural and ancestral conditioning may not be like this. They can be in momentum form; like story or movements and gestures, habits and cycles of behaviour.

Just as Heisenberg showed, one can measure accurately either the location of something (in space and time) or its momentum (= velocity x mass); where there is no beginning, end nor any form of location. Or, both can be measured approximately. The same seems to be true for human measurements; traumas are coded either in space-time (the left-brain relativity) or in momentum-flow (such as stories - right-brain).

There are seven different kinds of intruded trauma, and three which relate to genetic inheritance and the cultural field, making ten in total. As usual, the seven follow the structure of the seven days of the week. The projective trauma described so far is a Sunday type, relating to intrusive trauma.

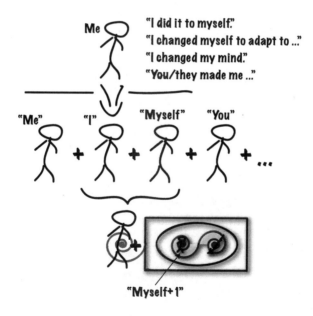

Adaptive trauma

119

The Monday trauma is self-inflicted, normally in response to adapting to the world around or to one's own internal cultural collective. The Tuesday trauma relates to learning and development, including missing learning, mis-learning and false learning.

Wednesday trauma relates to identifications; the roles and personas, the mask and character worn and played. Thursday trauma is simply behavioural and can be easily changed with simple approaches, like NLP or CBT[54].

Friday traumas relate to death, letting go and attachment. These are serious in the western world, and perhaps the biggest cultural problem we face. Saturday trauma equates to inappropriate needs or desires, often sponsored by traumas in earlier cycles, or inherited issues.

5.2. Gateways and Doorkeepers are SIGNALS

"The door was open, so I walked in."

Involuntary responses, asides, gestures, grunts, coughs, comments and feelings are signals from the client system that do not come from the directing (present) consciousness. They come from the aspects "frozen" in time in the measurements made, and the represent the attractors, both internal and external. These are the client's system's "messages" the facilitator has to notice and act on; maybe to feed them back, maybe to note them for completion, or maybe to put together the picture of the client's history.

---

[54] Cognitive Behavioural Therapy

The consciousness is trapped in a world view and limited physical space, with no awareness of what lies outside its boundaries. It will judge, misinterpret, get annoyed, disrupt and generally attempt to sabotage the attempts of the rest of the system to become conscious. Why? For the same reason that people in power want to keep their power – they fear they will disappear or somehow be less without it.

Like all fears, this is illusory. The consciousness just expands and becomes more powerful for being integrated with the full resources of the person. But fear is a strange animal that misperceives the world through crooked lenses.

Gateways are patient – if you miss the signal once, they will signal again and again and again. They are the symptoms. The symptoms are the system trying to do its job right but failing. The task is to help the symptoms do their job. This is quite like homeopathy, and definitely the antithesis of allopathic[55] approaches like collapse anchoring, squashes and sending resources to the inner child. The gatekeepers are the signals representing the entry points for change.

So, rather than fighting or alleviating "symptoms", we see them as "signals" offering opportunities to help the system to heal itself. Everything happening is considered to be signals, and all signals are considered to be "from the not here and now". Our evidence for this is a consistent result that once a person is sufficiently present they find inner and outer peace; there are less and less signals that disturb their system.

Peace is the signal of the void of "no mind". The symptoms are the system trying to heal or make sense by re-creating the precise geometry and environment so that they cease being stuck. Often though, the signals are not understood as such, so repeated experiences re-layer more of the same on top of the initial "trauma".

---

[55] "Allopathic" is the conventional medicinal approach, including many psychotherapies. It is about suppressing or deleting disease or symptoms, like using aspirin for a headache, whereas "homeopathic" works with the symptoms. Holigral is homeopathic, and disavows allopathy except as a very short-term fix as part of a programme to work with the symptoms to heal the client permanently.

If too much happens it might result in a dominant feature[56], or even a "black hole", with its event horizon [57], equating to the edge of an OCD fixation[58] or a stalker acquiring his target [prey]. From this insight comes one of the reasons for "working with the symptoms"; what benefit would there be in conflicting?

However, there is now an interesting dilemma. After many defining moments, the original signal meaning is lost and the present self is definitely not associated with the past self of the signal. The present self may react badly if presented with such raw feedback and so, from the facilitating point of view, I do not point out the real meaning of the signals, but rather I work with the communicating and the present perceptual reality.

As processes like re-scaling unfold, finally the client is in a position to perceive and understand their own system and their own signals, and then they can lead their own journey without any further need of a guide.

Because the facilitator knows the nature of such a journey but not the content of the individual journey, it is very much right to consider the facilitating role like that of a guide accompanying an expedition. They will not know the territory, but they can help with how to navigate; they have a good internal compass for the direction to "El Dorado".

I identify three other kinds of defining moments in relation to the perceptual position of the moment, in addition to the default "victim "perception. The perpetrator will also be affected, potentially losing life force into the victim. A witness or rescuer might also experience a dissociating, and so might a person be affected by being told the story of a trauma.

One example of witness trauma was a child told off and warned that they would be punished by their father when he came home. To the child's horror, the mother told the father "to sort out that child", and his elder sibling received the punishment. Another example is one that happened to me when watching a film. I acquired a fear of dogs from watching "The

---

[56] Dominant feature: like a very large planet that swallows others, or a star swallowing its planets.

[57] There is no escape from a black hole once something is within the event horizon. Once an attractor fills the entire being there is no space left from which to try to escape; the wormhole is the only way.

[58] OCD fixation; Obsessive-Compulsive Disorder.

Omen". In that instance I was associated into the character, and took on the fear projected into him. Scaling the emotions cleared the fear. Another time, I was affected by a newspaper story of an abuser that ended up killing a child. My empathy for the pain of both the child and the perpetrator caused me pain for years until I addressed it.

Facilitating the work requires to understand the entire life's journey from the perspective and scale of the self at each moment, from before conception until after death and from all the world views of witness, perpetrator and victim - and more.

5.3 Monday Processes

The themes are measurement and adaption. Social judgements and inferred perceptions of others are a fertile ground for self development, so the first process is aimed at deconstructing cultural belief systems.

The second part addresses forms of self-defence against projections, which are safe adaptions. These avoid the kind of adapting that incurs the cost of creating personal structures.

5.4 Deconstructing Cultural Belief Systems

"The transient and the eternal are different in essential nature."

In the spring of 2009, exploring more into gradual conditioning, I decided to label the more instantaneous defining moments as "digital" and to label the more ongoing and ever-present fields of environmental or cultural forces as ·

"analogue". With these came a host of cultural conditioning information, like cultural defining moments[59], cultural pronouns, and ways to apply the personal pronoun work to cultural pronouns.

Much of analogue, being ever-present, is of momentum form - because momentum has no location in space or time, only direction/flow, and so I started to develop the analogue forms for undoing the cultural and for working with the dynamics of relating and relationships.

A person can get the feeling that they are "complete" or "at peace" when they have addressed their internal pronouns ("protons"). However, the cultural influences can be subliminal and overridingly important (missing unresolved "electrons"). This is a counter-projecting process applied to oneself.

Actually, it is less a process, and more about giving some options about addressing one's "electrons" in world around. For those who have largely addressed the inner world (of "protons"), merely asking one of these questions seems to lead directly to the perceiver owning the perception, and a greater sense of being one with the world around, being the world around, causing the world around.

These cultural forms of conditioning have a way of developing that may not be due to one single event, but rather to a series of events or to a continuous field or a gradual projecting. Therefore, I call these "analogue forms" of conditioning. The emerging moving process also applies to undoing cultural conditioning (Chapter 8).

Questions / Instructions	Comments - Variations
And how could "they" be comparing "themselves" to others?	"they, them, we, us, people, someone, no-one, nobody, everybody, folk, humans, ..."

---

[59] The Berlin Wall, Independence, Hastings 1066, The Battle of Britain, are examples of cultural defining moments. Cultural pronouns are words like "society", "people", "they", "the government".

And [now] how could they be "judging" [themselves/others]?	"comparing, judging, feeling, thinking, perceiving, sensing, wondering, analysing, criticising, justifying, "
And [now] what could they be thinking "about" ...?	"about, to, with, from, ..."
And/so "now" ...	"now, then" - varying the temporal index for now or past/future.
And "how" could ...	"how, why, what, when, who" - these vary the index of the source
And [judge/compare/...] that again.	This can be combined with the active question.

Cultural beliefs are pervasive and unquestioned, as a rule. They are not even noticed unless one experiences a sufficiently different culture. For example, "I'll do it now, in a minute." is a perfectly normal and logical phrase that a Welsh person might use (in English), but an English receiver of these words might be completely mystified as to what has been communicated. So, a cultural field is present for everyone who grows up.

These are pernicious habits and ways of being that can be subliminal to the person doing them. Because they are potentially analogue, not digital in form, the way of addressing the work has to use both momentum and object-orientation.

The difficulty is identifying and feeding back the right challenge and then to move into a present-continuous source-oriented awareness. The forms of question above seek to do this by referencing the cultural "other" pronoun and asking in the continuous present.

Transcript

[Start of transcript. This transcript, being with a volunteer, starts from my asking about my topic that I have intruded that the client is likely to have as it is a common cultural thing. But this is just my excuse for not waiting for the client to start, and for intruding "compare". I also started with a generalised question, not a specific behaving form, so I got the consequences.]

So, how do people compare themselves with others?

They look at body shape and clothing, height, are they fat or thin, are they much fatter or thinner, do they look attractive, can I look them in the eye, are they too attractive for me, are they too ugly for me. I don't like revealing myself like this, I would not want other people to think I thought these things.

So, how else do people compare themselves with others?

How clever, how good they are at something, I don't know that everyone compares, you know.

So, how could a person be comparing themselves to another person?

They might not be, I've just realised I've been judging others not comparing them with me at all. It is not right to assume people compare.

Okay, so how could a person be judging other people?

[Scratches nose, makes a face, scratches head.] You want a verbal answer?

Yes. How could a person be judging other people?

By making assumptions and treating them as if they were true. [flounces their hair]

How else could a person be judging other people?

My immediate answer is there is no "how else" that's how it works.

Ok, so how are they making assumptions and treating them as if they were true?

Well the human decision making process seems to be take what information you can gather and come to conclusions about that. So, I guess that, um, people jump to conclusions based on too little evidence and they fill in the gaps with story. Eventually those stories become true for them, not necessarily for the people they are judging.

Ok, so how do they do that?

I suppose by that you refer to filling in the gaps with story. That's all tied in with the phrase "must be" which is all assumptions about um what must be going on for somebody else for them to behave like that.

And how are they assuming?

Because people needs explanations they need reasons and if they can't find the reason in truth they find one for themselves, it might be wildly wrong but it has to at least be plausible.

And how are they doing that?

By trying out different scenarios and seeing which one fits the available data best. Some people can base their whole opinion about another person, on their assumptions about them, and they go on to treat them as if their assumptions are true for the rest of their lives.

So where does assuming come from?

It's the process by which we make sense of the world right from the start that's how little children get their ideas about things and as they grow up they learn more about facts so they revise their assumptions to more closely fit what is accepted as the truth. Its the human default model of learning.

So where could that have come from?

[Head shakes, shrugs.]

Okay, so how do you know that this is the human default model of learning?

Through observation of lots of young children, hundreds of them.

Okay, and how do you know this to be true?

I only know it to be true for myself and all the children I've observed, because without exception they have all followed the same mechanism. I mean making the assumptions is a natural process, its what we do with them that's really important.

Ok, so how are people dealing with their assumptions?

Well there are two camps really. There's the camp that treats those assumptions as true and acts accordingly, and there's the other camp that just treats them as assumptions or knows them to be assumptions. They are a bit more restrained perhaps. They wait for more data.

Ok so it there anything else about that?

There must come a point in a child's development where they move over from a state where all assumptions are true until proven otherwise to a state where they realise assumptions are merely hypotheses and can be proven wrong. So I guess that a person's reaction depends where on that scale they lie.

And is there anything else about that?

I don't know, everyone's entitled to their own way of doing things. We can't tell anybody else how to behave or how to react, that's something they will change if they want to, not because they are told to.

So where does treating assumptions as true come from?

That's the little children experience. Most children gather far more information. They have to make sense of it so quickly and adults cannot explain everything to them and so they have to come to their conclusions and treat them as true because they could not hold all of the uncertainties and possibilities that that many hypotheses would involve. Perhaps they just don't get the opportunity to question every single assumption.

So how do you now perceive how you perceive the world?

I quite often jump to conclusions too quickly. And I get angry on the back of those when I don't actually need to at all. I can be quite an impatient person though, so waiting for more evidence that I may never even get is difficult. I think what's most difficult about that is that sometimes I'm required to act based on too little erm definitive [pause] evidence I suppose is the only word. Um, in the past I've got decisions wrong because of this, and then been blamed for it when to me its not been my fault, so it puts me in a position that I don't like.

So how do you now perceive how you perceive the world?

I don't know. I do know that for some things I only require a single event for me to be jumping to conclusions about people's motivations, but in other cases I'm quite content to wait until either the situation has blown over or I have enough information to feel confident about acting. I guess there must be some similarity between the trigger episodes.

So how do you now perceive how you perceive the world?

Well it looks like I've still got some work to do. I suppose the only comment that goes with that is that I've got very high standards for myself. I accept things in other people that I don't accept in myself.

Thank you.

[End of transcript.]

5.5 Self-Defence

"Queen's Gambit, declined."

This is an application of counter-projection concepts, designed to stop a projection in its tracks. Therefore there is a long list of how manipulators open their forms of influence. The easiest solution is to stop something before it even begins, because the Socratic Method is difficult to defend against, otherwise. It is always in the starting frame and assumptions that problems lie.

Bullies

With bullies and threats or menaces, simply tell the most useful authority figure. Most bullies are afraid of "bigger bullies". Sometimes the authority figure is not obvious, but it will be a person whose opinion of them is important to the bully. If someone is trying to control another person, they will probably used one of the "manipulator's opening gambits" - see the table below.

The initial defence is to say no to all suggestions; "Thank you; not right now. I'll think about it." Or return the compliment; "I invite you to consider that this is one hundred percent your reality."

Socrates would take an opening statement that was seemingly true on the surface (but actually not) and then lead his victim on an irrefutable chain of logic that ended up with the person agreeing their original statement was wrong. The Athenians showed their appreciation of this by making him drink hemlock to execute him.

Popularised by Plato, and beneficially used to understand the nature of things and to challenge prejudice, this has a dark side: collateral damage through embedding blame and shame in another person.

The attacker identifies a passionate statement/story that you have made. and plays the "I am with you on this, my brother, at the moment" game. Then, at a later stage, they put the statement into a different context and link it to your responsibility. They identify a "way in" by choosing something with truth or passion: a strong statement (passion) that you cannot easily disagree with, they place it in a different context from its original one, that puts the blame on you.

For example, a coach says "Players get hurt; that's just how it is". The manipulator says: "would you accept that it is possible that, in your role as coach, you are unconsciously not showing proper concern for the safety of your players by showing that attitude." This feels like an almost undeniable request to take the blame and emotional inferiority.

This would then be followed-up with a series of other statements that lead progressively to self mistrust, and therefore dependence upon the manipulator as the "honest broker", thus destroying the spirit of the coach - all apparently in the name of "the greater good". The simplest defence for the coach is to intercept the first "pass" of the manipulator: "No thank you, I decline your suggestion".

By defending oneself and others, then all can start to freely exchange ideas and thoughts, and a virtuous circle gains momentum in place of conflict.

A systemic way to minimise manipulation and maximise performance comes from how to achieve globally optimal performance in a large organisation. The answer is pure simplicity and can be applied even to governments and sorting out global issues.

Every team is rewarded for its own performance, but its leader is rewarded for the performance of the team of leaders as a whole; thus the leader counterbalances the team needs with those of the world around, at every level.

This would imply that CEO's work together for the industry and that boards deliver the results for the individual companies, and that presidents work as a team for the whole planet, and are rewarded only for global results. Their cabinets are rewarded for national performance subject to the global constraints, represented by their leader.

Opening Gambits - and Some Responses

Reflecting back the gambits is the simplest defence option. Stopping something before it gathers any momentum is the easiest way to address an attack.

Opening Gambit	Comment / Response
Let me put to you ...?	The "let" is asking for permission; once given the manipulator has the power.
	"Thank you but I do not choose to let you."
<Name>, [pause], I invite you to consider ...	Using your name is an old trick. The invite is a soft way to make a person accept. The "consider" is also a gentle step, so this trick is about gradually pacing the embedding of something into the intended victim.
	"No thank you <their name>, I invite you to consider this for yourself."
I suggest that you ...	"Please keep your suggesting to yourself."
I put to you, that ...	"I put this back to you, that this is yours."
May I put something to you?	"No you may not."
There is ... in you ...	"So in you is ..., is there?"
You are/have/do/ ...	"So you have ..."
Would you accept that you/your ...,	"No, I do not accept."

Opening Gambit	Comment / Response
Trust me, ...	"Why should I trust you?"
Maybe you caused ... by ...	"Maybe I did not."
With ... respect, ...	"I did not ask for this. Stop, please."
Are you with me?	"That depends."
Thank for for agreeing listen to me, ...	"I do not agree to listen."
Would you give me the power to ...	"No."
What I'm hearing is ... "you" ...	"That is your opinion."
I don't feel heard ... / listened to	"Indeed I do not."
In my judgement ... you ...	"Please keep your judgement to yourself."
I would suggest ... that you ...	"Please keep your suggesting to yourself."
Might I suggest ... you ...	"No you may not."
That's manipulative ...	"Takes one to perceive one."
This is not a safe place ...	"Then please make it safe for me."
You are resisting ... / avoiding / denying / refusing / not listening to me ...	"Of course I am resisting when attacked."
There is no room for me to speak ...	"I would like room to speak."
You are interrupting ...	"Of course, I do not want to hear this."
If you wish to ...	"No I do not."
If you'd like to ...	"No thank you."
Have you ever known me to be wrong?	"Yes."
One thing that concerns me about you/your ...	"These are your concerns."

Opening Gambit	Comment / Response
Don't let me interrupt ...	"Okay, I won't."
You said ... (in another context)	"You have changed the context of my words."
Would you agree / admit / accept that ...	"No."
Perhaps you would ...	"No thank you."
Would you not agree...	"No."
Do you ...?	Defer. "Why are you asking?"
Would you like to consider that ...	"No, would you like to consider that you ..."
Consider that ...	"Thanks, I'll take it under advisement."
Maybe you are / could / have ...	"Maybe and maybe not."
Believe you me ...	"Er, I do not."
Having one's words turned around, especially using something that is felt to be true, like "You are too dependent on other people's opinions", is difficult to defend, so realise they are always talking about themselves.	"Yes I often do, so now you are depending on others' opinions in this instance."
Accept me as I am.	While this is a mantra for healthy living, these words can also be manipulative, requiring that unacceptable behaviour be condoned. So all rules have exceptions! "I do accept you, but that behaviour is outside of what I am willing to experience."

133

Opening Gambit	Comment / Response
Divide and conquer. Here, a person talks to many involved people, individually, convincing them each first, using words purporting to be from the others, to get consensus on what the divider wants. "John says he wants to go to the zoo tomorrow." (When the speaker Joe, not John, wants this!)	Sometimes called "shuttle diplomacy", the good side of this is used to keep face given difficult decisions, and to avoid public disagreements. Do not agree to anything before all others involved are also consulted by yourself.
"Framing." A manipulator sets a narrow context (frame) on a discussion or statement to get their way.	Decline the opening frame. You probably know something is wrong but cannot "put your finger on it". Defer any discussion until you feel clear and find the problem.
They may also set a different frame on something you may have said in one context, generalising it into their chosen context.	If you feel rushed, confused or disoriented by a person then also suspect manipulation. Slow down, refuse the rushing and allow clarity to re-emerge.

The defence is to say no initially to all suggestions. It is fine to ask for opinions about projects or goals or the business, or things external, because they are not about "you". How would this change a performance appraisal? It would focus solely upon goals and targets, and what the manager / company needs to do to help you do your job. In other words, turn appraisals completely upside-down!

5.6. Chinese Whispers: the six degrees of distortion?

One thing tickled me, and it perhaps relates to people interested in deception. I emailed a friend about a topic, and received a phone call from another on the same topic, but somewhat distorted. I checked the circuit of people in between, and coined the phrase: *"Six degrees of distortion"*

I wonder if there could be a mechanism of gradual retelling of events or stories that establishes an emergent, different version, and whether this might be one way people lead into self-deceptions, and Freudian defences.

Because this is well known in social networks, under the phenomenon name of "chinese whispers", if the equivalence of six degrees of separation between people on the outside is true on the inside, then chinese whispers would maybe hold true between different aspects of a human being.

Something happens; a person justifies, rationalises or creates an internal explanation. Then they build a belief system around that in order to make the explanation true. Then something else happens, and the response to that has to take into account the prevailing belief system, and therefore, they develop a distortion at every level - potentially a rather worrying scenario for the sanity of normal human beings.

5.7 Monday Summary

How the world is measured or judged has an effect on the world around, through how the "electrons" respond to the inner protons, even if it is only "in the mind".

In August 2007 I decided that I'd like a dog; just to keep me fit by giving me no excuse to avoid a morning walk! So I decided on a labrador retriever, either chocolate brown or golden. I met with the rescue people and they "vetted" me. I said I'd be back from a trip on the 13th September, so I'd like one on the 14th. The lady said "so I'll start looking from the 15th." I said "no, the 14th". She gave me an odd look, but nonetheless on the 12th I was called to find I had an appointment to meet a golden lab on the 14th.

I visited the kennels, arriving noticing a strong smell of dog urine. In my mind I started to judge the keeping of the place, and as a result the gatekeeper nearly bit my head off. I realised he was a security-alsatian archetype of person, and apologised in my mind. He came back all sweetness and smiles, having been energetically recognised, and I took "Sam" for a walk.

He pulled and pulled on the leash until I was back at the kennels. I then turned around to walk away again; the leash relaxed, he looked up at me, as if to say, "I'm with you now", and trotted happily alongside me. Then the lady tried to insist we would collect Sam a few days later. I was having none of this, and sure enough she brought him to my house within the hour, while I visited a pet shop to get initial supplies in.

His reputation was that of ripping things apart and wild, but when in our house he just settled well, happily playing ball. So we went into the garden and he just came and sat down alongside me. The lady's jaw was down to her chest, and she left saying, "Well, he's still going to need some training". Very funny.

So, I was advised to keep him on leash for several walks and only to let him off the leash on the homeward section once he knew the route. Needless to say I did not take this advice and let him off on the outward walk first time out. He ran ahead, and my son asked, "What happens if there are cows in the field?" I replied, "Then he will trot in, see them, circle round and return to us at the gate". Sure enough, he did.

The dog follows precisely the owner's projections, and so it goes with teams, such as in sport. The order of influence on winning comes from the owner, then the coach, then the captain and finally the team.

All these actors needs to be in a certainty of winning; or losing will happen. But the single most important energy is the real leader of the entity, whether it is a sports team, a single player or a coach or the manager. The person who leads is responsible for the results.

Now, back to the dog. The dog is a mirror, and I suggest any person who desires to be successful gets one, because he is the most faithful mirror and giver of signals. Early on, my dog would walk eighteen to twenty yards ahead of me, consistently and I wondered why. Then I realised that after twenty-three years playing club cricket my focus of attention was typically the distance between batter and bowler. Immediately, I was able to unmeasure this and he then walked alongside me or at varying distances.

Of course, his favourite game was fetching the ball, seeing as cricket was my game. For a long time, my dog would drop his ball next to fragrant piles of dog faeces. Nice. But finally I got the message - and this one took me years.

The message was simple; dogs exchange information by smell - from each others' behinds, from each other's faeces and urine. Humans do the same; they trade information through stories. Yes, everyone has a story, and the matrix works by trading stories. The moment I got this, he stopped dropping his ball in such aromatic places. This was a habit the dog had for years; gone. The result speaks for itself.

You can tell almost everything about a person from their dog. Therefore, manipulators will rarely have a dog, as it gives away too much unsavoury information. I make it a rule to be more careful around non-dog-owning people.

If a sports-person has a dog, then the dog will tell them everything they need to know in order to acquire the winning mind set. And it will tell them everything they do not want to know about their subconscious "loser".

The key learnings are:

- self-defence,
- keeping clean of projections,
- understanding the signalling of the world around,
- addressing one's own projections in the moment.

6 Learning

6.1 Stories

The Tuesday phase of the cycle is all about learning, the land, stories and making sense of the environment; a process called sorting. The best ways of learning involve metaphor, analogy and stories to transfer knowledge about the world. This is why fairy tales are so instrumental in making children beware the dangers of the world. There is great truth in these stories, and I have seen almost all the major archetypal stories at play in clients' lives. People do live out the stories, albeit unconsciously for the most part.

Increasing Subtlety

So far we have only considered primal defining moments, largely based upon emotional fields; and not even all aspects of that. We have also to consider the layering of more subtle effects as people "grow up".

After the foundations of energetic and emotional power have been set up, the next phase to consider is learning; linguistics, early years, early schooling effects, and the most unsubtle social shaping - I am *assuming* that social shaping becomes ever-more subtle as people grown up, because a learning classifier system[60] adapting to the world does exactly that; get the world approximately right and refine, refine, refine.

Communications Theory

Play, and communicating through play, is the layer of most natural social influence; tactics and strategy. Relating, communicating, making an initial sense of the world around, puzzling out the strange logic of these giant

---

[60] A learning classifier system is a form of Artificial Intelligence based upon systems of neural networks that is designed to handle "perpetual novelty"; literally to learn about its environment with a minimum of pre-coded functions. See the work of John Holland for more.

beings who give such conflicting messages, associating the sounds known as words to experiences, people, contexts. The beginning of acquiring a labelling scheme happens, in the form of language: "mamma", "dada", "good", "bad", "naughty", "well done", "go to sleep", "eat all your food", "play nicely", "NO", "okay", "yes", "nighty-night", "light on", "light off", "nappy time".

Communicating is a shaping of the projecting-sensing, where perhaps a specific focus now determines how the person's energetic antenna beam pattern is shaped[61]. The primal energy of connecting energetically is now overlaid with emotional variety, sounds, words and then word patterns, developing eventually into conversation.

The topography shapes this learning phase; are there similar-sized beings with whom one can share this strange experience of being among giants? Are there slightly bigger beings who "know the ropes" and can show me how to survive this strange world, or do these slightly bigger beings do painful things?

The world of the only child can be very different to the world of the child with a host of siblings. One has two primary significant figures to track, the other has a whole host of complex goings on to make sense of, but also more company like to be of a similar and a more mutually-communicable age.

The physics of communication is dominated by the "bandwidth" of the channel. There might be a lot of high-frequency, subtle information being sent in words, but the child's receiver may only be able to grasp and differentiate the lower frequencies, as they are in the business of developing their very general but powerful neural network (brain), and have yet to develop the discrimination.

As the coarser signals are recognised and processed-out, so the brain can assimilate the subtler signals. This process is also fractal, as reflected in the trees of evolution that we make of categories of life.

In a signals intelligence system, sorting is first coarse and then refined as sense is made of the coarse information. Clusters of signals are grouped, and then once enough information is gathered to be able to separate the

---

[61] An antenna beam pattern shows the relative receptivity to different directions. Normally the main focus of attention has most of the awareness, and little from outside of the focus might enter awareness. Extreme focus can make a person oblivious of danger, for example.

coarse groups, the content of the groups are sorted into finer categories, and so on, making a fractal learning of the world. As before, the chaos principle of starting conditions predominates, and the nature of the learning, adapting and conditioning will distort or shape the understanding and communicating accordingly.

For most people, the adapting of the neurology eventually trains onto a single language, and the ability to learn others will depend on how the first language was learned. The neural patterns will shape the ability to generalise, associate and construct a new language. But it is not just the words. I had the opportunity to learn French as an adult, through complete immersion into France, and I recorded the journey's path of acquiring the language.

A couple of examples illustrate my point. Spoken English has a wide range of accent and tonal variation, so the english ear and voice are tolerant of these variations. The consequence is that the english ear will be potentially deaf to the subtle variation of a language that has very little tonal or accent variation. French is just such a language where the markers between words are completely different to English.

After about eighteen months I found that I had retuned my hearing into French, and I even started to speak English in a French way; because it was easier on the French ear in meetings that were multi-lingual. Literally, the dynamic range of in-word sound levels and tone variations feels an order of magnitude larger in English than in French, and the brain tunes into these kinds of bandwidths, because that is how the child learns to optimally engage with his world around.

The post-script to this is that it took me about eighteen months back in the UK to re-acquire my natural English voice variation.

On the play side, the roots are set down for games; how to play them, how to recognise them, and how to find the role that seems to fit what "I" and "the others" want to play. The primal games seem to be: "peeka-boo", "hide and seek", "tag" (or "it'), "king of the castle", "winner-loser", "sleeping lions", and "pass the parcel".

Story-telling, especially of the fairy kind, tells about the wider range of more sophisticated (to the child) games available, and roles move into the archetypal "hero" and "journey" forms.

Beyond these are then overlays of increasing sophistication, revealed in the kinds of play, films and stories enjoyed: from hunter to detective or criminal, from pantomime to comedy, from warrior to sportsperson, from "kiss-chase" to the romantic, from disappointment to tragedy, from trading children's game cards to "business", and so-forth into career and life roles.

What can science observe or say about all these layers of sophistication? We can observe the structure that holds this in place and how the measurements are made. We can infer how to un-measure at any of the levels. We can equate forces: attraction and repulsion, action and reaction, and we can observe the sophistication of the "signals intelligence system"; which perhaps is the key benefit. We can bring in gravity to assess social standing, we can bring in relativity as people evolve into their maturity, and we can use quantum physics to understand separated or differentiated states of being.

The meta game to understanding the world around or clients, is to gather and understand the intelligence picture; in this case, this relates to the games being played. While the Transactional Analyst might have their specialist knowledge for the less healthy games, it serves anyone to be able to read and play everyday games to their own advantage, as well as to help the others playing possibly unconsciously. Working with a game can help it to complete. Once it is fully understood it no longer holds a fascination.

In fact, the Holigral Method has emerged from studying normality, with only the occasional brush with so-called "abnormality", and understanding normality is a key life skill in our social world.

6.2 Sorting: the Sense-Making Function

The sorting[62] system is also corrupted by mis-measurements and by any developing blind spots in the measurement system. Depending upon the nature of the errors, the sorting system can be incredibly robust to them, as the process of sorting naturally has much redundant data. Outliers can then be readily discarded when developing a taxonomy for characterising the signals and their sources. The very process requires a level of "noise" errors to function well, which is provided by the natural variation of environment.

---

[62] Signal Sorting was my specialisation for seventeen years, and I feel that I either have to write a book on it or just leave the fairly cryptic summary of a vast field of expertise.

The kinds of environmental factors that cause problems to the development of a robust human sorting system include things like "low diversity", "system overload", "the absence of normal cultural learnings" (such as a modern child not growing up with television or books or music), "complex clusters of signals that are difficult to separate" (such as "too much variety, too soon"), "incongruences between the parameters from different sensors" (such as feeling hostility and lies but hearing "good words"), which last is an example highly likely to develop a paranoid complex.

The actual signals of relevance for the growing child are:

- boundaries - the rules, the edge of how closely they can push the rules, which is a kind of boundary flexibility; danger signals,
- the cues for the roles that people play, and the appropriate signalling of these roles, and how and when roles switch,
- the games and stories that people are in, giving a landscape and a more sophisticated set of rules of engagement,
- the tactics and strategies of these games and stories.

As the child develops, he-she learns ever-more sophisticated versions. But as with the sensory system, if there are distortions or errors in learning in a primal game, like "hide and seek", then the consequences are more and more difficult to redress when playing the more sophisticated games; perhaps even impossible.

If a person learnt only to hide, and not to seek, then their choice of roles leaves them predisposed to secrecy and a difficulty being open, and if a person only seeks then they may have difficulty holding secrets, and may not place themselves where they can be found.

Eventually they may reach a level where they make their own game, and rules, and seek to involve others. New games will attract those who are bored with the old ones. Understanding the game being played gives insight into how to operate in a job.

For example, recognising that the modern social worker is really an insurance broker playing the game of insurance makes all the roles clear. The customers are the general public (many with mental health needs), the suppliers are the doctors, counsellors and alternative health providers, and the claims assessor and financial controls are all separated from the broker, who is the intermediary. While the activities are more complex in social work, the model of the insurance game keeps the roles clear and simple, making everyone's job easier.

It is almost impossible to meet a person who is genuinely free of any kind of game or role or persona. Even the Dalai Lama plays his role in the game of enlightenment. To engage in the matrix is to engage in games; the fun is in raising the game to as high and as sophisticated level as possible, enabling world change for the better. Even if it is in the local community or at home, it is making a difference.

Boundaries are critical in pattern recognition systems[63]. If they are too sharp then black-and-white splitting happens, if they are too soft then many decisions cannot be made. There is a "just right" nature to healthy boundaries in recognition systems, reflecting the same with humans - flexibility combined with clarity. Some rules are strict, some can be bent and some broken, depending upon the context.

Sophisticated decision-making software may make use of a theory called Dempster-Shafer[64], which is based on "fuzzy set theory" and the idea of combining two measures: probability and plausibility. These two measures give independent votes for "yes" and "no", respectively, and reflect the complex decision making in humans. Doctors use expert-system decision trees for their diagnoses, and this approach is copied in Artificial Intelligence systems.

---

[63] Boundaries are the decision surfaces of classifier systems. To minimise error rates, one requires regions of "no decision" and to avoid critical areas where a slight shift in data makes a significant shift in its classification. See Chris Bishop on Neural Networks for more information.

[64] Dempster-Shafer theory addresses two-fold factors in decision making and tracking: combining the probability on one axis with the plausibility on the other axis. Zadeh's Theory of Fuzzy Sets gives the underlying mathematics.

6.3 Tuesday Processes

The example processes from the Tuesday, contextual form, address sorting and insight into the story playing out in one's life. The emergent result of these processes is "right understanding", just like the Truth Process, but now by using the natural engineering process of de-interleaving, and the situation awareness that results from understanding a story and how it relates to one's life.

6.4 De-interleaving

"Sorting out your life."

Having Re-scaling, the Truth Process, and Pronoun Scaling, I was still wondering as to other ways of working with the client to most easily attain "Right Understanding".

Wanting to work with large systems of pronouns and signals, and recognising that a lifetime of accumulated signals was coming from a client, it made sense to go back to my roots in sensor signal processing algorithms and situation awareness systems[65]. These systems receive signals all jumbled up from the environment. Pulses from different radars arrive at a sensor, and the sensor has to measure, sort and understand the nature of each radar's signalling, and to identify its source.

All of the processes in this kind of system, in which I had been expert for sixteen years, applied now to de-interleaving the signals from a single human being. Literally, I could re-apply the stages, the processes and the methods, and take a client through a process that helped them to become "situation aware" with regard to their life.

---

[65] These are systems that are designed to work with perpetual novelty, making sense of electromagnetic environments in particular, to protect high-value assets like ships and aircraft.

In other words this was another way to become "at one with one's environment". While the process looks complicated from the outside, everything within it has simple steps and simple logic.

It assumes that all the signals happening now, which are (mostly) from the past, are all jumbled up and trying to communicate. To make sense of this, one has to collate, sort and re-assemble the signals until a complete picture appears that makes sense. One is then at peace because all the signals have been heard and understood.

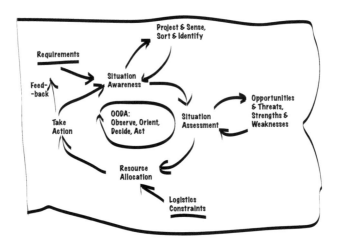

The Situation Awareness Cycles

The overall process is:

- Gather information
- Cluster information according to a metric representing similar pronoun ages or styles (colours used, handwriting styles, ages of drawings[66], ...)
- Sort the information by pronoun

---

[66] To understand signals, one has to recall and understand all the phases and ages of development of childhood, such as the order in which different kinds of drawings emerge - face first, then head with arms and legs, then adding hands and feet, then a body, then figurines, then stick people, and so on.

- Identify the pronouns (scaling or truth processes)
- Refine and merge or separate pronouns as required
- Add or collect more information as required
- See the whole, identified picture of the personal structure, as it is.

The idea is first to collate enough information to start: write down every sentence, every statement, notice every significant life event, notice emotions and body signals. One way to start is to "represent the story of my life", but to divert to this process after the first telling of the story. Or this process can interact with the full story busting.

When enough has been collected, each sentence has to be separated and then grouped according to which ones "go together" - perhaps by "pronoun age", or "colour" or "age of handwriting or drawing", or another criterion. Gradually the grouping can reflect either different ages or different people's words or some other grouping, unique to the person doing the process.

At this point, maybe more signals have to be collated and allocated, maybe new clusters of signals are needed, maybe sets of signals are related and others are not. Maybe some signals readily relate to aspects of self and maybe some signals come directly as from another person (for example, like a parent's voice being heard inside a person's head).

Once each group has been formed, it can be sourced, and the origins or roots discovered, using the Truth process or Pronoun Scaling, for example.

Questions	Comments
Write down or represent everything and anything; every belief, every common thing you say, everything; your life story.	Any thoughts about yourself or others or the world around.
Keep on writing; have others notice what you say to them, and add these sentences.	One way to begin this is to write the story of your life - at least once over.

Cut each statement onto its own piece of paper. Then place together the sentences that come from the same pronoun.	Can use post-its for each statement. A pronoun is the term for the myriad "I, me, you, myself ..." Assess each group and subdivide or collate as needed.
Add any more statements that go with each group, and place into their own, new group any statements that fit none of the groups.	Start to become aware of the age and context whence each group comes, who they came from before, and beyond.
Sort and identity the sources and roots of each group, until you are clear on how each of these came to you in the first instance.	Trace back sources enough, and the right understanding may well bring humour, the cosmic joke and joy for the rest of your life.

The process works incredibly well, to reduce a whole life into a few days, if the client had the ability to organise the information through sorting processes. It also confirmed the right understanding and a similar/same effect as re-scaling on the whole-life level.

The problem really, is that the facilitator probably needs to understand enough of the signals and the information as to suggest possible clustering options. Each client being different, the way of partitioning the data accordingly is subjective, and therefore can become less clean in approach. So, even though I was the world's leading expert in sorting radar signals, I rarely use this myself.

6.5 Story Insight: Recognising Stories, Roles and Games

The first aspect of developing any new skill is to raise the awareness first. In this case, the key skill is recognising and working with the games to allow them to complete. The patterns to recognise are the games, the stories and the roles others are playing. Knowing the game gives a complete insight.

The model is that the culture of the world around uses archetypal story and game forms as the basis for how people interact. The cues, the roles, the scripts, the outcomes, are all rooted in stories and games. These are healthy; not the unhealthy games of "transactional analysis", although these are also present.

The simple basis of story and game is created in early childhood in interactions like "peek-a-boo" and "hide-and-seek". Increasingly sophisticated overlays are then added as we develop. By understand the stories, the games, consciously, you gain the advantage is knowing more what is going on around. You are more "situation-aware", which is a key aspect of warfare, but also a key aspect in achieving your goals in life; knowing the present lay of the land.

Questions	Comments
"What is your favourite film?	[or book, story, music, game, poem, TV programme, game show, hobby or internet site.]
[Take your first, instant thought; first answer - however ridiculous or inappropriate.]	It is important to choose the real, inner favourite, not one that you might choose so that another person might think well of you. It's not about "choosing the right film" to be seen socially well; otherwise the process will not work.
Write the names of the main characters, each on a different post-it. Place each post-it in a different space.	Make sure you have the space to "visit" each post-it physically; by being able to physically move to each space.
Identify the role of each character. Visit each character to understand their role.	Add the role to each post-it.

Where are you in the movie; which scene?	This tells you where you are in your life.
	This is probably you.
Which character do you most identify with?	They will be there; take the time to recognise them.
Who in your life represents the other characters?	
How do the characters complete the film?	
What is the classic ending of this type of story?	This tells you how it ends, and also how it can change while still respecting all those involved.
Are there any other possible endings?	"Which rules can be bent, broken or not?"
What little changes might be possible?	
How can you use this film to understand the story going on around you, right now?	Be in your role.
	Respect the story; this is real life.

Transcript

[BEGINNING OF TRANSCRIPT]

Take your first, instant thought; first answer - however ridiculous or inappropriate.

"What is your favourite film, or book, or story?

Cinderella. Not just any Cinderella, this is the Cinderella from the "well-loved tales" book that I had when I was little.

Write the names of the main characters, each on a different post-it.

Place each post-it in a different space.

[Wall, doorway, and fireplace and not labelled but easy enough to locate!]

Cinderella obviously here [by the fireplace, then places all the others].

Identify the role of each character.

[Sighs. Yawns.] Cinderella did everything for everybody else, but wasn't really at all appreciated for it, or, rewarded for it.

Father brought the wicked stepmother in but did not support Cinderella from what the stepmother was doing, didn't protect her.

The wicked stepmother was the one with all the power, and all the control.

The ugly sisters were there to make Cinderella's life miserable.

Fairy godmother was the rescuer, first person who was really on Cinderella's side.

And Prince Charming was Prince Charming, he was the happily ever after.

Visit each character to understand their role.

I don't need to visit that one, I live in that one. [Cinderella] I mean parts of this story are no longer relevant to me, but parts still go on, other parts happened to me as a kid. Here, I feel injustice is the biggest one, but there is also "it goes on forever", incomprehension, and a sense of being closed in, into a much smaller world than other people inhabit.

[Father - opposite end of room] Inability to stand up to the stepmother.

Wicked stepmother is backed up by the ugly sisters, and stands between father and daughter. Strangely I don't have emotions or feelings in this place [the dog growls - a most unusual thing]. A feeling of being like a spider in the middle of a web, here.

Ugly sisters - they are there to fill in all the gaps, they seem to be everywhere. Their main role is as tormentors, and they feel just completely self-serving, they don't care about how anyone else feels.

Fairy Godmother - closer to Cinderella than any of the others, so far. Comes in from a different direction, of course. She's able to reach out to Cinderella and pull her away from the influence of the other characters.

Prince Charming is out there [another room] because he is in another world. He's actually - the fairy godmother is directly in a line between the stepmother and Prince Charming. So as soon as Cinderella comes around this corner he is ready to take her off completely out of sight of all the rest of it.

Where are you in the story; which scene?

Ah, two places, one is right at the beginning, where there is no hope of anything for Cinderella apart from a lifetime of servitude, and the other one is right at the end, there are a few nice stopping points in between which involve pretty ball-gowns and things.

Which character do you most identify with?

Cinderella.

Who in your life represents the other characters?

Okay, so, um, my dad would be the father, my mum the wicked stepmother, a whole load of bullying girls in school were the ugly sisters, my grandmother was the fairy godmother, and my second husband is Prince Charming, my first husband failed abysmally in that job.

How do the characters complete the story?

Well part of the story we know how it completes. The fairy godmother comes unexpectedly into Cinderella's life, and protects her from the wicked stepmother, then eventually Prince Charming appears and carries Cinderella off into his much nicer world. As for the other characters, the ugly sisters have long gone, the wicked stepmother and the father have grown up, have changed beyond all recognition, and there's no longer any sense of persecution or controlling-ness or lack of support.

What is the classic ending of this type of story?

Happily ever after for the main character, and some kind of "just desserts" for the baddies.

Are there any other possible endings?

There are a variety range of possible endings for Cinderella, varying degrees of gruesomeness, but Cinderella always gets her Prince Charming.

What little changes might be possible? [ask if necessary.]

How can you use this story to understand the story going on around you, right now?

It's not just right now, its how its impacted my past. My childhood felt like an eternity of unfairness.

The only way that the Cinderella at the beginning of the story and me in my childhood were really linked was through that unfairness. I didn't have to do lots of jobs around the house, it was just the unfairness of what was going on for me, that really resonated.

Now, um, as a mum, I find myself doing jobs continually, nonstop some days, just like Cinderella was supposed to have before the fairy godmother showed up. At least the unfairness is gone and I have my Prince Charming. All the women in my family have worked hard, this is the in-service part isn't it?

[END OF TRANSCRIPT]

The purpose of this process is not to "fix" things, but to reveal what is happening. The client then has choices. They might choose another process to work on the "doing jobs continually".

6.6 Learning Difficulties and Autism

Roots

If we consider the roots of the word "education", it is latin, *educare*, meaning "to draw out". A very strange thing is that most modern education is about pumping people full of as much information or knowledge as possible. However, the next economy will be insight management, and insight comes from empty minds, not those cluttered with facts and figures, because a flow requires an empty channel to best flow through. The modern age, demanding ever-reducing timescales, means that business will have to follow the martial arts into flow states of peak performance, such as "no mind".

Flexibility, adaptability, stamina, endurance, reactivity and ability to achieve goals are the keys to success in the coming years. The key to these is to eliminate blocks, limitations and difficulties, and then to expand consciousness through learning ways of perceiving from many angles to attain a holistic perspective, leading to the most effective actions.

It is time to return to the real roots of the meaning of education, and draw out the unique talents of each student, for their best and for the best of the world. The aspects of education specifically addressed by Holigral to date are:

- learning difficulties - nonlexia
- autism, attention-deficit-disorder and other behavioural problems
- peak learning states, particularly attaining and maintaining "no mind"
- generic processes to gain insight and understanding of a subject
- learning life-cycles and good learning habits

Learning Difficulties

I visited Plumpton College in the UK, for two days, to work with the learning difficulties coordinator to help students suffering a wide range of forms of dyslexia. The college comprises about 2000 students and staff, with sixty-five percent having learning difficulties. The coordinator, in a few weeks, transformed the college; there are no longer difficulties, the students are able to pass the exams and the staff know how to set work so that the students can complete it.

> "Nonlexics often don't hear or relate to what is being said or they misinterpret what is said. Since they have access to the equivalent of a 3D home entertainment system in every waking moment which is so habitual and natural they rarely know their gift.
>
> I suggest they have a choice to turn off this entertainment or inner dialogue whilst listening, writing or reading and then tune it back when they fancy. Up to them. Nothing is wrong, nothing is right, which = freedom = calm = being understood = nonlexic's no longer need to show the lexics the maze, so hares off!!! And finds a new game.
>
> To hear, learn and implement ideas they need to believe in the tutor and vice versa.
>
> Since Holigral coaching techniques I truly believe in students ability to achieve what they wish too. And so it is....
>
> So then their phobia's towards reading writing....... can unravel."
>
> Julie Sellars, Learning Difficulties Coordinator, Plumpton College, UK.

Autism

The autistic spectrum is wide, far wider than the normal spectrum, but mostly autists have a lack of embodiment and a missing understanding of the normal social matrix. We address this by processes to integrate emotionally and spiritually, and educating as to the nature of the "normals". We also help them to realise and use their special talents that exist because they are not entranced into the normal social matrix.

Peak Learning States

When subject matter is presented at the right time for the student, learning is effortless. The single biggest factor that we have observed in learning performance is the attitude of the teacher. If the teacher radiates that everyone can be a star, then the students will reflect this. If a teacher judges or radiates any negative emotional charges during learning experiences, then the students will similarly reflect that in their performance.

There are simple self-modelling processes that we have, that help students access their peak learning states and recognise poor learning states and what to do about them.

The Lifecycles Model also applies to learning patterns, just change some questions from using the word "relating" to "learning".

Nonlexics and Peak Learning States

"Not understanding own difference. Not knowing own strengths.

Confused by others confusion. Others are confused by our ability to `get" the world although we ourselves are unconscious of what we knew until the unlock of Holigral.

Fear of being perfect or normal or in control (they feels very familiar at the mo])

What is fact and what is fiction?"

Julie Sellars, Learning Difficulties Coordinator, Plumpton College, uk.

Lexia and Nonlexia

I define a "lexic" as a person who has acquired the serial-reading programme, the word-by-word experience of the tortoise, and who is therefore associated into the world of step-by-step progress, goals and results; left-brain, cognitive, relational. They are dissociated from the hare world of the nonlexic and autist.

The nonlexic hare is entirely the opposite; right-brained, intuitive, highly emotionally connected and responsive, which makes them vulnerable to the harsh, judgmental environments like schoolrooms. They easily absorb and therefore confirm the projections of the teachers, because they are so sensitive, and thus prove them right by failing on reading, writing, spelling, maths and generally academic subjects.

The first issue is the classroom emotional environment. At defining moments of learning trauma, the emotional field of the teacher and the group is installed into the nonlexic, and they then repeat and deepen the non-functionality.

A nonlexic only needs to read the key words to understand something, as they do not need sequence. Whereas a lexic needs sequence and a "story in the right order" in order to understand something, "cat sat mat" has an inherent logic that the nonlexic understands. The little words mean nothing to them, and they become traumatised when the teacher forces them to read pre-positions and articles like "the", "on", "and" and "a". [Non-lexically; little words mean nothing. Become traumatised teacher forces student reading little words.]

One of the main causes that we found for the rise of nonlexia is the loss of the comic strip from mainstream educational reading curriculums. The comic strip is a vital transitional step between the pictures-plus-some-words to the mostly-words, and while many students can make the big jump, others will fail. With the comic strip, the transition is more successful.

The comic strip is also a vehicle to improving sentence construction and comprehension for those with reading or writing difficulty. By turning each word into a symbol or glyph or picture, a sentence can be turned into a picture or a series of pictures. This enables the nonlexic person to capture the meaning. By placing the words on the glyphs, the sentence can be matched.

The complementary process is to draw an idea in comic-strip form, place words on the objects and verbs or pre-positions accordingly, and to then sequence the words. By taking the sequence back to picture form one can cross-check the compilation. This strategy has worked for adolescents with severe reading and writing difficulties.

In relation to this, the Mayan glyphs took my interest. The first time I really gave them attention was using the metro in Mexico City, where the stations are all signed by glyphs, with only small writing underneath. Clearly in a culture with many tongues, a common symbolic language works, as long as you know what the symbols mean.

This led me to looking at the Mayan symbols themselves. Predominantly, they are series of front-on faces. The basic language is one of emotional sequences. Clearly, for a dissociated, scientific world they will be difficult to read, but at the emotional level they become self-evident. The modern-day emoticons of e-chat software are a move in the same direction.

It became apparent that the teacher's emotional state during learning is the biggest cause of learning trauma. The expectation and unconscious emotional judgements of the teachers set the students' performance. The only answer is to completely accept all students as perfect, and to move into independent learning for all students; a huge paradigm shift in how education works.

One example of accidental learning trauma involves the moving finger while reading. If the teacher points at one word at a time, the child will associate the pattern of the word with the left brain, whereas if the finger is moving along the line then the right brain engages and the momentum form of measuring is incurred, resulting in the letters moving/jumbling if reading is then attempted without a moving finger.

The nonlexics are literally pushed into the margins of society; society is associated into the text and lexic, and the outlaws, outcasts and rebels are literally marginalised (in the margins of the pages). The Wizard of Oz rules the world; the certificate signed by someone with a more important certificate is what the lexic sees as important, rather than the actual ability. Luckily, the worm is turning, and the abilities of the nonlexics will prove invaluable to the future of mankind.

6.7 Tuesday Conclusion

Story intelligence navigates the social world. One can begin to get a deeper understanding of the social world by recognising the cues in the clothing, jobs, house, car, figures of speech and even phrenology as people grow into their roles, which is the focus of the next chapter. Everyone is associated into some game or story, sometimes many, and people unconsciously play out the roles accordingly. By reading the signals in the moment, one can change the games, change the story lines and escape tricky situations better.

7 Identity and Recognition

7.1 Icons, Image and Brand

What are these seven icons representing? Why are they designed as they are?

In Autumn 2009, I happened to be in Mexico City, and I took the underground metro system. I was immediately taken with all the stations being signed by icons, not with words. Clearly for a multilingual society that may not be literate such icons work really well to indicate the places, as long as one can correctly interpret the icon, although that is not easy for the modern, left-brained human. Just notice how much difficulty they have with understanding hieroglyphics; Egyptian or Mayan.

It became apparent to me that the Mayan face-on glyphs communicate emotions; the language is formed of sequences of emotions. The Egyptian patterns are also symbolic, and as with letters, one symbol can have more than one meaning depending upon its context. The last thing these icons are, are solely phonemes. That is the booby prize, and probably wrong.

Why not represent a story in symbols rather than words or pictures? There is a concentrated meaning to a symbol or glyph or pictogram. The spaces can be explored using either scaling or perceptual space, and story-busting can be used as an alternative. Fourth, you can tell metaphorical stories, or enact out resonating dramatic forms, working with archetypes, which are metaphors for aspects of personality.

The main benefits of metaphor, though, compared with other approaches, are for transferring learning, understanding, and communicating.

Metaphors are probably the most efficient form of thought virus - think of the parables and bible stories, fairy stores, jokes and gossip; metaphor travels well. As people naturally understand metaphors, then pictograms and glyphs representing cultural metaphors might be just the right form for universal quick message transfer.

The logo will say everything about an organisation to the person who can understand the logo. At the deeper level, they have a huge effect. For example, British Telecom used to have "Busby", a yellow bird that was cheesy but loved by the general public, keeping the company popular. At great expense, the logo and colouring were changed, to a grey, "high-fluting" character. No surprises then, that this alienated the general public and began the inevitable decline in popularity.

7.2 Wednesday Processes

The two identity level processes address common problems; insufficient sense of self, and a lack of connection to one's personal power and charisma. The first process, called "Rock Solid", is designed to grow up a self after intruded structures have been removed, and the second, called "Reclaiming Power", is designed to regain what I call the "sperm principle"; drive and will-power.

7.3 Rock Solid

I noticed some clients who needed a stronger sense of self even when completely full of life force, as they had no boundaries. They had never had a sufficient sense of self earlier this life. This process will progressively build a self with foundations of rock; it creates or finds a core strength, something the Japanese call "Getsumi no michi".

The idea is to wind back time using a micro "pulling-back" process until a factual descriptive experience, and then move forward again. This process is not appropriate until the deconstructing and re-associating has happened, which normally takes place on a retreat. Doing this with a highly dissociated person will be very factual, but as a defensive experience, not the real thing.

Question / Instruction	Comment
Choose a scenario or person or thing that you will be meeting or addressing or interacting with in the future.	Or choose "me, here and now".
And as starting/entering ... now what is happening as starting/entering ...? And NOW what happens? [And is anything else happening?]	Use 2-3 questions for the 2.3 sampling of whatever is being sampled. For the above start, "and as me, "here and now'-ing, now what is ...?
And as that [last answer] is happening, now what is happening as that [last answer] is happening? And NOW what happens? [And is anything else happening?]	Ask this pair of questions 5 times. These are addressing momentum-flow and object-relation, respectively.
And what do you know now? And what knowing is emerging now?	If there are loaded words / problems noticed in the responses fitting well-adapted forms of the anthropological pattern then use the modified "pulling back" process (next process).
And what happens just before/after/in-between ...? or And what is happening just ...?	Slow-down time using ... to find the precise sequential place to release/change/undo the old patterning and upgrade with a new choice.

Is a statement ...?

       conditioning: (incoming / installed from outside)

       adapting: (choice to change for others)

       or developing: natural understanding/factual.

Depending upon this understanding, the direction is either backward or forward in time. Going back in time uses the following sub-process.

Pulling Back Process

This is used to slot into the Rock Solid process when it is time to explore sources and get back to before the starting conditions of a problem statement.

Question	Comments
1. The client makes the problem statement	The starting pronoun is declared.
"And what was happening just before you became like this/that?	
2. "and what was happening just before [that]?"	Until it becomes neutral enough pre-problem (3-5 times probably), or until the dawn of time or beyond.
"and what was happening just before ...?" or "And what was happening just after [that] and before ...?" "and then what happened?" / "and then what was happening?"	Use the in-between time modelling to find the perfect "ordinary" starting point, which is a fact, not a problem. or "And what kind of you were you after ... and just before ...?"
3. "And as ... is happening, now what is happening as ... is happening?" "And now what happens?"	Move forward in doublets - unless a problem state is encountered. Until "here and now" If a problem state is met, go to step 2 and return to step 3 once it is resolved.

Sometimes the client will jump between times. The missing elements can be found using the "in between" questions. Sometimes it can pay to use a little pronoun scaling to clear an emotion that lies between the "factual" description and the "problem description."

At least three, probably six, layers of pulling back are required, and any adjectival qualifiers mean that something is not pristine.

This process is a quick and elegant solution to many small problems in life.

7.4 Reclaiming Power

Sometimes, people play victim in a highly unconscious way. Rarely are their "persecutor" actions or the things one has done to others brought up and addressed voluntarily on retreats. But without balancing this, the relationship with the world around will be unbalanced, naturally; the free electrons will wreak havoc.

Excuses, complaints, justifications, stories and reasons are all ways where power is given away to "the external world", whether it is to another person or traffic, or any other excuse. We already have the story-busting process to address these patterns, so the point here is to identify the role and the identity being taken on when such things are happening.

This can be highly annoying to the client, and needs a good, trustworthy relationship before use. The point here is to challenge, by naming the role of precisely what is happening, like "victim" or "giving power away". Power is often given away in an interaction.

Questions / Comments / Instructions	Meta-Comments
The clients makes an excuse or comment or complaint or goes into a story-telling mode.	Notice the energy loss of power; where it flows.
Name the behaviour or the role, e.g. "victim", "excusing".	Gently challenge. Keep doing this.

Name the pattern, name the giving of power: "giving your power to the excuse [again]."	Keep doing this, for example naming a pattern, like "Sissyphus", or "Tantalus".
Name other patterns, like "distracting", "diverting", "stalling", "complaining", "justifying".	Keep naming what is happening.
Are you willing to take responsibility for everything that happens?	Keep asking, and keep chasing down excuses or stories until affirmatively yes.
"Let the anger flow, go inside it" ... 6 times! or	Wait for the client to become VERY angry and ...
"what has to be true for ...?" (Truth process)	release the anger and find the power of the true self within its core.
Then accept you have your power, and no-one else can take it unless you give it away.	Check this is accepted.

This appears "unclean" from the normal perspective of facilitating Holigrally. However, the purpose and the needs are very different, in terms of bringing the unaware projected energies back into the body, and in particularly in safely re-integrating the "sperm principle" once the egg is fully embodied - a kind of "safe ego".

It can be facilitated the normal, clean-navigating way, as all that actually needs to happen is to re-associate the aspect; the life force of will. Once embodied, it is IN. So this is a short-cut for a specific purpose. The normal processes will also work for integrating the will, as long as the anger can be accessed. So, provoking the response to invoke that gateway would be appropriate to enable a client to re-embody a dissociated will, but is clearly not appropriate for any other client issues.

As with all Holigral processes, this is working with the client's symptoms and would only be undertaken at the client's request. Otherwise, the facilitator is likely to be on the receiving end of the client's justifiable wrath.

7.5 One Identity

The purpose of the Holigral processes that undo structures is to reduce the collective self to unity consciousness, and to expand this to a sense of oneness with all that is around. However, without an adequate sense of self this may not make for a functional experience in the world.

The enlightenment principle proves to be feminine - the egg. This makes sense of Buddha initially choosing only academic or wealthy men for his monasteries, because men needed to learn the feminine principle at that time. The only disease is seriousness, and the only problem was over-egoic self.

By re-integrating the self after enlightening, a healthy ego is created. The modern person often has the sperm principle dissociated in service to the nanny state. Recovering this is essentially the correct last step in personal development. Traditions that do this earlier will need controls and codes to moderate the strengthened ego.

8 Flowing

8.1 Thursday Processes

While this is the day of process, tactic and strategy, it is also the day of habits, of flows and the perfect timing for momentum processes.

By Autumn 2007, a piece of the jigsaw that I had known to be missing a long time was signalling to me: momentum. The defining moments addressed by David Grove had been instantaneous - at least relatively - and based upon space and time. I felt that Heisenberg's Uncertainty Principle applied somehow. This principle stated that "one can measure either location or momentum accurately, but not both at the same time". I felt the location had been well explored, but momentum not at all.

I started experimenting with question patterns that undid defining moments measured in momentum. Initially, these were location-based emergent questions until they became self-referential in momentum terms. At this point the processes also had to be worded in momentum form, and so did the word "momentum", because as a word, it was object-oriented. "Momentum" became "moving-experiencing" and the processes became entitled "emerging-moving" and "inging".

These moving-experiencing processes were undoing long-standing physical habits like limps and postures, and were profoundly effective with PTSD[67]. I turned to combining location and momentum for defining moments when both partially held the measurement.

This also signalled the end of looking at just defining moments, and a move into considering "epochs" of change, gradual adapting and conditioning - working with plasticity, and patterns of signals. This needed a new

---

[67] I worked with some travellers who had been abused by police attacks many years earlier, and taught one of them to help the others. The results were a remarkable and complete loss of police phobia. The problems seemed to have been completely erased from their being.

approach that could deal with larger numbers of little events, and many more signals.

Momentum processes are right-brain in nature and intention. There is no beginning nor end, nor places nor locations, but merely flows. The processes shown here are:

- Emerging Moving
- Story Busting

The Emerging Moving process addresses physical habits, including gestures and limps, Tourettes syndrome, uneven gaits, and so on. For the facilitator and client pairing brave enough to face it, I believe that the inging can address and undo anything. The Emerging Moving forms are less a set of processes, than a range of ways of facilitating momentum healing using inging and emerging moving.

The Story Busting marked a new level in ease and power of working with clients. A person can literally map out the story of their life and come to right understanding after six to seven iterations. It is strongly advised, though, to also work through the story of the world around and the story of one's relationship with the world around in parallel with this story process, or one stands the danger of having relieved all the "proton" attractors but none of the "electrons" - and all hell will then break loose in one's life.

Before launching into the processes, though, first I represent the development of the thinking and logic behind this work, using the words I documented at the time, as it is special and very different from normal reality and perceptions.

Its power is deceptive and it is worth being prepared, as the effect of working with it cannot but affect the facilitator also.

It might prove puzzling to read this chapter, because the form of the language might dissolve the self-other relating, making it difficult to stay reading and having a recollection of what is being expressed. I'm sorry, but that is part of the point of the Momentum: to give access to "the other side of experience".

8.2 Musing Emerging Moving

There are many ways in which information stored as movements or habits can emerge. It may be found in a particular way of walking, or in a gesture, or a repeated movement, or a posture. In almost all cases, we are not even aware that we are doing this thing, and we are certainly not aware of the amount of information that it is holding for us.

Through this we can access all kinds of hidden knowledge, releasing ourselves from places where we are stuck, and returning to ourselves resources that have been locked away for a long time.

If my very language re-measures moving experiences (a nominalisation[68]) into objects then my very language has to be different if I am not to immediately re-measure - to avoid losing the flowing of moving emerging.

So, a completely new language - not even a language - "languaging" is required to enquire and to facilitate. Or rewording, it is requiring new languaging for facilitating for emerging moving knowing - wow!

This requires moving from object-oriented (OO[69]) measured language (normal English) to processing moving (the English equivalent of native American).

In OO speak: adjectives like "a" and "the" have to be eliminated from the languaging, and so do the non-moving prepositions (after all, they are Pre-positions - a pre-posterous notion from moving-perceiving frame-ing), so the languaging is becoming (does "is" staticise/measure?) verbalising "gerunding" as sequences (sequencing). Of course, it is also non-stationary so OO minds have real trouble initially grasping the languaging and the meaning - and that's ok, so am relearning to undo OO languaging and move into human being/doing rather than "a human".

---

[68] Nominalisation; the linguistic term for a noun representing a verb. This is all-too common in the English language, to the detriment of clear communicating.

[69] OO = Object-Oriented; the wording comes from a form of programming based upon the objects, whereas the early languages were based upon the flows. Personally, I always preferred flow-programming, and with hindsight I now know why; I was a creature of momentum.

There are measured locations and measured movings, and it is only "un-measuring" that is required for "healing". The aim is to be moving from a "fixed, or periodic moving" to "non-periodic movings", for example;

> from tapping fingers to flow,
>
> from eye tics to smooth movement of focus,
>
> from limping to walking.

After a physical trauma the body freezes muscles and compensates, and after mending the muscles unfreeze, to some extent, but the adapted postures and movings have affected the habit. The emerging moving is to undo the habit.

This is rather like Feldenkrais[70] but not manipulated by a facilitator; instead it is self-re-learning by the "clienting". One client, with forty-eight years of limping after a bad knee injury, cleared his limp in five minutes using the emerging moving pattern.

To start to make sense of the emerging moving from the normal perspective of object-oriented consciousness:

> 'I" measured the moving trauma (verbs) into "nominalisations and OO form", and after understanding this, I can unmeasure by emerging.

Once all structures are un-measured, there only is moving, and a new languaging is required by occidental human beings to stay unmeasuring and in flow with life ... well that's a start for a Sunday (Sunday being the day of trauma measurement).

The indo-european languages are the direct cause of losing connection with the Tao[71]. When we speak we measure into object-oriented forms due to the spatial nature of the languages of Western Europe. Now, are there other languages (other than native american) that work in flow, but certainly

---

[70] Feldenkrais - check it out.

[71] Tao Te Ching, Lao Tzu.

Russian and Hungarian have more flow, being languages of horse-people in origin. So, too, are there the languages of dance, ballet and music; mostly captured by the "dots" rather than the spaces in between.

This does indeed go back to Adam and eating of the tree of knowledge - knowing comes from measuring. It is true therefore, that before knowing (or outside of knowing) is Eden. So, Eden is the Judao-Christian form of enlightenment, but its not a place, it is a flow of four rivers.

8.3 Emerging Moving Process

"Keep Moving"

Questions / Instructions	Comments
Choose the movement that you want to find out more about.	You may decide to ask about a repetitive or habitual movement or gesture, or just choose something seemingly more at random, such as a way of walking or dancing.
"As I am [movement verb]-ing, what knowing is emerging as I am [movement-verb]-ing?"	The languaging of the question keeps the experience "in the now", and keeps it open-ended. This way, the information can emerge as it requires to, and keeps emerging until you stop.
Keep asking this question.	Until the moving is changed satisfactorily.

Alternatively, as you are doing the movement, keep asking yourself, "And now what is happening?"

This is like a game of join-the-dots, where you are simply noticing one thing after another. These may be physical sensations, memories, movements or anything else that you notice. It is not necessary to analyse each one; simply acknowledging its existence is enough, and then ask the question again.

Keep asking this question until you find that you are just getting on with something else.

Once the signals have emerged and been acknowledged, they have usually cleared the initial signals so effectively that you will have no memory of there having been a problem.

The process also applies to cycles of patterns of behaviour or meeting habits or time management habits like procrastinating, e.g. "And as I am procrastinating, now what is happening as I am procrastinating?"

With cycles, sometimes it is worth pausing and noticing the whole cycle and applying the perception to the whole cycle rather than the initial parts that are revealed by the questions at first.

8.4 Story Busting

"Undoing the tyranny of the narrative."

Another way of dealing with large systems of pronouns emerged through the momentum form in September 2007. I realised another way of dealing with one of David Grove's principles. He had this idea of "the tyranny of the narrative", where the client tyrannises the facilitator and other people with their "story".

Story-telling is a moving-experiencing, and so being a momentum form, I tried this out, "tell me the story of your life", and then "tell me again, please" - six times. After a few trials, I had discovered that this simple process could consistently free the client from their story. By working WITH the story, its purpose was completed, and it ceased to be.

An important knowing that is the corollary of this is that once something's purpose has completed it is no longer needed, and it stops. Problematic symptoms are signals, and once heard and understood they stop. My mantra became: "Nothing exists without a purpose, and everything else has one. The purpose of "nothing" is to exist without a purpose." I called this "Story Busting".

Story is a momentum experience because it is a flow; a person is taken on a journey by the storyteller, literally "there and back again", to quote Tolkien. With sufficient sensitivity a person can literally feel the flow and the pull of the story. Conversation and verbal interaction can become a flow as the relating grows and the self takes a back seat. When conversation does not flow, people are more self-conscious and less relating is happening.

Applied with pen, paper, writing and drawing over several days, the process could enable a person to become at one with the internal aspects of themselves, addressing the internal protons, but missing out the electrons of their projection onto the world around, with a resulting upheaval in life.

So, I developed the complementary "story of the world around", to balance the personal story, and then the story of one's relationship with the world around. All these three were needed to balance and undo the flow-momentum as a whole. We also developed derivative forms of story busting, including processes to work with over-analysis, excuses, criticism, justifying, and dream-busting, during the spring of 2008.

Other stories that you might like to work on are: my career, key events or experiences, my ancestry, my culture, my business, my team, my family, my country, my religion, my beliefs, my dreams, etc.

Stories can be represented in so many ways: in metaphor, in prose, in poetry, by comic strip scenes, storyboards, in words, in mime, music or dance or sounds or pictures or fusions of these.

The important thing to remember is to allow the story to express however it needs to express, and to keep retelling the story until the teller makes the realisations that mean the story is no longer needing to be told. These realisations may take some hours or days to fully emerge after the telling of the story, so we normally take plenty of time to go through this process. This way, the client is fully supported throughout. Sometimes the story just needs to be really heard - once and fully, and sometimes more; flow with the client's story's need.

Questions / Instructions	Comments
Represent the story of ... and represent the story of the world around ...	Balance is essential, and so addressing the inner and the outer is one way of doing this.
Does anything else go with that? And anything else? And what do you know now?	Is there anything else about that [story]?
Represent the story again OR Represent the story of that story.	Repeat the above process six times - including the story of the world around.
Alternatively, you could use: Tell me the story of .... Sing me the song of ... Chant me the chant of ... Act the play of ... Orchestrate the music of ...	It can be fun to do this while out for a walk - or in bar, late at night, or to go somewhere atmospheric to experience it. Choosing a different space or posture or angle for each telling also adds something.

Another option is to tell the story from the point of view of different actors, and the narrator.

Story busting works at the chunking level of the person's experience, given the time and scope of a session. This transcript was a forty minute session, clearing a dislike of using phones. Phobia would be too strong a description. Notice how the story shifts as layers of perceptions and events are revealed, and the client naturally makes their own sense. This is, from my point of view, one of the easiest, yet most empowering and effective ways of facilitating a client to a real result.

[BEGINNING]

"I don't want to call them."

1 Tell me the story of not wanting to call them.

Ouch, my ear hurts - its a real ear-ache. I mean it really hurts, and I don't want one, and I don't like speaking to people when I got to complain, and I don't like bad feelings, and I don't like speaking to strangers, but I am ok speaking to people I know, although I still don't like complaining, and I'd prefer someone else called them, can't you do it please, you are so much better at calling people and relating to them than I am [puts on a big smile].

2 Tell the story again, please.

I don't know where to begin. [Pause.] I grew up not really using the telephone until my first real girlfriend. I think we had been told not to answer the phone as younger children because a stranger might be on the line. Mum said sometimes strange people call and say nasty things, so don't answer the phone. Maybe I got a kind of negative feeling with that, maybe when I've got to speak to someone who might not like what I'm saying they will speak, well I feel like a small child, I don't know what to say, and I want someone else to speak. Ummm.

3 Tell me the story again, please.

I think it goes back to fear of strangers, I now remember that mum also said to be careful after school and not to get into cars with strangers, and I've also had a big fear of hitch-hiking, so I think it goes back way further. Do you think she might have been afraid of strangers, and we kind of got it from her? Hitchers put out their thumbs, but that used to be a big insult - no, biting thumbs was, forget that, I'm confused now. Where was I? Okay, yes, I think there is more about giving bad news, and a vibe of this being kept quiet, like its not okay to talk about bad things. And I think this might come from grandma, or mum, why do I feel like this is to do with grandad's death, I was only very young then, maybe mum got that news on the phone. I don't know, I know its irrational to not want to pick up the phone to speak to a stranger, I guess I don't need to be afraid anymore, but how should I be? Umm - [smile] again.

4 So, tell me the story again, please.

Okay, so [pause]. Here I am, a call to make. I can do it now, but I still feel a funny feeling in my stomach. It's not nice, I feel like burping or sicking up some mucus, like I've swallowed some. Yuck. [Rubs around chin]. I've got a metal-like taste in my mouth now, like there is something unpalatable to say. My jaw aches, I feel head-achy, I really really don't want to use the phone, at all, right now. Can we do this another time? [Big breath.] It's kind of sickening, like were phones only really used in the old days for emergencies like booking an appointment to see the doctor. Maybe the phone was used mostly when we were sick, so then we'd see the doctor, or maybe the dentist. Maybe the phone did mean a bad experience was on its way. So is there anything about the kinds of phone call I don't like? I don't think so, it still feels like strangers, but business [pause] or is it? I do take my time to get round to calling the doctor or the dentist, it can take months. Okay, so I'm procrastinating, hoping it will all go away. But I know it won't, so I usually get someone else to do it for me. What a palava! It's so silly. But why?

5 So, tell me the story again, please.

I also remember my father making all those calls during the recession, it was killing him, making sales call after sales call to no avail. I could see his spirit dwindling daily, he lost his heart I think. Overall you know I'm not at all sure that the telephone has been a great experience for me. I far prefer to send an email. But now I think about it, I'm fine going in and asking directly. I'm okay with people face to face, it can be difficult but I can deal with it. I think its about the facelessness of a phone. I think I'd use a video phone a lot more. Actually I do, I've started to use skype and I prefer to text chat or video. And I least like the voice only. It's true for me, I like to see people when I'm talking with them, and I like the eye contact, there is something about that, people can't lie so easily and I can read what's going on more easily, much more easily. It's why I like to buy at a shop or online but not over the phone. I'm actually okay with this. Now I know I'm going to see about this.

6. So tell me the story again, please.

It is just that, a story. I can do what I like, really. I prefer to meet people directly, or to text or email or leave a voice message. I can and will do it now. There's no problem now. I'll use my preferences and get on with calling when that's the only way. Thanks. That wasn't so bad actually, it's quite easy, quite freeing to know where your stuff comes from.

Thanks again.

[END]

The momentum processes uses the flow against itself, like a Tai-Chi move.

8.5 War and Peace

"It's a bit like a pair of fleas arguing over who owns the dog?", Paul Hogan – "Crocodile Dundee II"

An Absence of Peace

Let us start by defining conflict through what it is not: conflict is the absence of peace, harmony, joy, love, laughter and naturally-cooperative behaviours that benefit all. The scope of conflict is vast, so let us consider the pinnacles of conflict and the ways in which people have sought peace. In this chapter I consider the worst case of the consequences of conflict: war and warfare; from within the self, in households, through tribal disputes and ancient warfare, to global nuclear warfare, terrorism and the war on drugs in the modern age.

After over five thousand years of primarily conflict, I believe that humanity has experienced enough of that, and it is now time to give peace a chance. This section addresses the fundamental issues involved in conflict and in creating a peaceful world that has all the benefits and none of the perceived losses of genuine peace.

The philosophical frame of reference is "no sacrifices": if there has to be a sacrifice at any point and at any level, then we are not working with the system in a way that will lead to a permanently effective peace. This means that any enjoyment from competition, sport and life that is presently achieved through conflict still has to find a way of satisfying the primal urges and needs of the humans partaking and observing.

In a very natural way this is already happening where, mostly, youngsters who play out war and fighting in computer games have less need to play these out physically. Obviously there are exceptions, but just as the amphitheatre replaced tribal conflict with ritualised "games", so now are these needs being satisfied with an indirect substitute.

We live in a relativistic universe where every point has its unique frame of reference. This does not mean we have to live in conflict, but it does mean that we each have a different perspective. So the kind of peace we require has to be one where difference leads not to conflict, but rather to understanding.

How do I reconcile these seemingly disparate perspectives? How do I live in peace and with peace, and yet still have the vitality, the life, the richness and diversity of experience; without conflict as a naturally inherent part of my life and of the world around my life? How do I encourage peace around me without imposing it, without becoming some kind of preacher, without placing myself in untenable positions?

By seeking to understand conflict and peace, by using this understanding to take a wider perspective, and by then working with the insights revealed, a way is proposed towards a genuinely peaceful world that involves no sacrifices, either in the nature of the peaceful world, or on the path towards such a peaceful world.

What is our experience of conflict?

I remember one time at school, a boy picked a fight with me, in the queue waiting for the bus home. He attacked me off-guard, and hit me several times. Just as I was throwing my first punch a teacher grabbed my arm, shouting "No, stop", and the other boy was flung a few feet away. I stopped without having hit back. The boy was hauled off to see the headmaster, and I was left fuming and angry that I had not had the completion of getting a good punch back.

I spent the night dreaming, visualising revenge. The next morning, as I got off the school bus, there he was, waiting for me. I wondered, "was this for another fight?", and my adrenaline was rushing. But he held out his hand. I took it, we shook, and that was it.

After having had fights with the other boy for a year or so before this event, thereafter we lived in peace. My friends were angry at me; they thought I was being a wimp, they judged that I did the wrong thing; they wanted to see another fight. I was also angry with myself for "letting him off the hook", for "not having got even".

I remember thinking that this boy was a waste of a human being, and wished an early death on him. He died aged seventeen in a motorcycle accident. And I have to live with this. I am not proud of it, but the facts are the facts.

I had gone from a conflict with the world around to a conflict within myself. With decades of hindsight I can see how my beingness offended this other boy; how I had brought his attacks on me, and how by accepting him, in that moment of apology, he was released from further conflict with me. I was, however, cursed by my own judgement of him, and and have had to live with that. I see now that this was a crucial early lesson for me in accepting others and not judging them.

> Think of a time, in the past, when you had a conflict with another person.
>
> How did it start?
>
> How did you first become aware it was a conflict?
>
> How did it progress?
>
> What kind of steady-state did it have, if any?

How did you resolve it, or did you leave it unresolved, or how did it end?

What do you know now?

The symptoms of conflict are things like stress, battles and disease; whether it is a "war of words" or more seriously engaged. We can see conflict in almost every aspect of daily life: it is endemic in modern society. So how do we address something that is so ingrained, so "part and parcel", that we literally do not know another way of being?

What we can observe is that conflict is happening when two or more parties are present and not exhibiting the signals of peace. It is not much, but it is a start. These parties will have different views but somehow these views are not cooperating, love is not present, and neither are joy nor laughter in sufficient quantity to have their healing effect. Maybe respect, or listening, or something is missing in the seeking of understanding.

The underlying problem is not different views, but the separation of selves that have these different views. They do not feel "at one" at the deeper level that would result in a positive experience of difference. As the Holigral theory shows, separation comes from dissociation; the dissociation between self and other, which itself comes from a series of defining moments and epochs relating to the battle between Freud's "ego" and "super-ego". Conflict is one of the down-sides of separation.

The regime of duality and the separation of humanity from multiplicity, with the inherent good-versus-evil energetic defining moment, is a big factor. With this root undone, it is more now about enabling similar resolutions at the human level.

Ancient Egypt is alone in having had a religion of consciousness; no other religion shares this form, Buddhism being a philosophy. There are no swords in the royal regalia of Egypt, whereas other rulers have sword and mace. The mythology has been divergent ever since the Osiris myth was lost into the world of the "One God" and religions of duality, such as Zoroastrianism.

My desire is to recreate a newer version of Ancient Egypt, of heterarchy and co-operation. The problem is that such a society cannot survive amongst neighbours who worship war. The warlike societies have to be transcended from within, globally.

The Problem

The very problem for me, in even beginning to describe the problem of conflict, is "chicken and egg". Within the egg-world of conflict there are only solutions that return to another level of conflict, maybe providing a temporary peace. In the chicken world, there is a permanent, working solution, but the universe inside the egg knows nothing of the chicken world. I am seeking to express both the egg and chicken world views of the problems and solutions, the context and the chains of causation.

Solutions for enduring peace can only be seen in Tibet and Ancient Egypt. Everywhere else, conflict remained rife, and both of these empires eventually fell to the warlords of surrounding territory, albeit for different reasons and causes. Switzerland finds its remedy by having a national army and holding the wealth of the corrupt, thereby remaining inviolate to the otherwise corrupt ravages. Inside the egg world, the established solutions are:

- establish a common, external enemy
- one God
- one great king
- conquest
- genocide
- take over at the top

All these have weaknesses that result in a flawed solution, to different levels of effectiveness. The common enemy just recreates another level of conflict; the price of this internal peace is outer war. The "One God" myth is great, unless there happens to be more than one "One God" - thus the perpetual war between the many followers of each "One God".

The concepts of the Great King of Persia and the Roman Emperor worked for centuries, though each with weaknesses. The Persian problem was that other Great Kings make for external war; only a single worldwide empire can work. The Roman Empire was buried under ever-growing bureaucracy; the very size of state and control destroys the culture that supported its growth. The Persians had separated governorship from military control, both in terms of region and tenure; the Romans never learned this vital lesson.

Conquest has to be total, and nearly always includes "divide and conquer" models, creating internal tensions again. Genocide is both impractical and imbues the enemies with incredible fighting power as they realise they are fighting for their lives. Taking over at the top replaces one set of wolves for another set, newly greedy to feed. Conflict within is reflected in world around, conflict around is reflected within.

I am listing some of the problems within the egg-world, in no particular order, and definitely not all of the problems.

Growth

The "Growth Model" originated in the injunction "go forth and multiply", and still humanity's leaders seem to think that the only solution to present economic problems is "growth". But on a planet where the natural resources are strained, where we already experience catastrophic losses in animal, fish, vegetable and mineral resources, an ever-growing model will consume resources faster without replenishing.

Even if we go "off planet" and colonise the entire universe, eventually the growth model will fail and deplete. Scales of conflict will upgrade from county to continental to inter-planetary to inter-galactic and continue until a fundamental lesson is learned: balance.

Growth is the perspective of an adolescent or child culture: children have to grow for sure, but eventually the mature adult stops growing and settles into a steady state and finally retirement and death. Human culture has to decide when it is grown up. So far, few cultures have shown a willingness to embrace population control and balance; and the countries trying to manage this are seen as evil in the eyes of the child nations desiring growth. Growth is not the answer; managing life-cycles is part of a better answer.

Big trees have to fall, inspiring new growth in the open space created - for younglings and also for other trees around.

Inequality

The refrain of the leaders of the Peasants Revolt in England in 1381 CE was "when Adam delved and Eva span, who then was a gentleman?" This cry from the heart of the peasants represents an eternal truth: the anarchists' slogan "property is theft".

There is no logic to why some people should own more than others, no logic other than varied mechanisms of slavery that dictate that one person is worth more than another. Energy is supposed to flow between potential differences; and if it does not do so smoothly then eventually a voltage leaks and the circuit shorts; it breaks down. Thus it is with wealth; it has to flow from rich to poor, even if there are cycles of sometimes reverse flow as this happens.

Money

Money was invented to equate effort once we had activities indirect to food creation, as a way of balancing the effort contributed. Over time it has become polluted and manipulated, and its end is nigh. It is a symptom of scarcity; if there is enough then we can share and there is no need for money.

If we abandon money what happens? Only the regulation of scarce resource; material objects separating the rich from the poor. So money now only serves to keep the wealth wealthy, differentiating who can have which level of luxury. We need something new.

If we look deeper at the creation of money, we see a sense of scarcity at its roots - a sense that there was not enough food resource to go around, so people had to contribute to receive. We see the storing of food to manage variations in yield due to weather, and we see the beginning of strife between nomad and agrarian.

Essentially, the cities did not willingly share with the nomads, who had a harder life and a stronger will. As a result, wave after wave of nomads took over the cities, generations after generations, right up to the modern day, such as through the spread of Islam, the Mongol empire and the Cossacks of Russia.

We now see economic migration worldwide. The cause of the migration is the simple fact that the wealthy do not adequately share with the poor, whether it be nationally, regionally, locally or internationally. Historically this is the cause of much of the strife recorded about the ancient world.

One great mythological counter-example is recorded of the Pharaoh feeding the Israelites, although it is unclear if this was the Israelites putting a better light on the Hyksos invasion of Lower Egypt.

The aid that is given, however, hides the corruption of the elite in the poorer countries. I was once shocked to find that I had bought organic fair-trade coffee, only to find that it was from Ethiopia. This was a cash crop from a country where drought is never far away. And the only reason I can deduce for this is to support an arms trade.

Methods of power and control

"Divide and conquer" has been an epithet of growing empires since at least the time of the Persians, even if it was most famously quoted of Julius Caesar. Our world environment, particularly in the UK, is designed to control the masses and give massive benefits to a tiny minority. We are controlled through a few simple processes, below:

- Everyday speech is full of unnoticed negatives ("no, not, can't, but, however, etc.) that focus our attention on the problem instead of what we want. For example, prior to the second invasion of Iraq we even had a "Stop the War" campaign instead of a "Peace Now" campaign. This focus on the negative disempowers people.

- Schooldays with ridiculously high amounts of homework - even for primary school children - and the stresses of exams at all ages (on both teachers and children) teach us to be "busy bees". Accelerated learning has been around for over thirty-five years; knowing some of it would enable people to start education at eight and finish degrees by eighteen – and with very little homework!

- We suffer unnecessarily long working hours with red tape designed to slow-down time-effectiveness and to create "busy-work" with little business benefit and long commuting times. Most managerial jobs can be reduced to one or two normal working days per week through learning clarity of thinking, sensory acuity and flexibility of behaviour.[72]

- Control is a management function, by definition, and is present to regulate flow in engineering systems. However, there is an inherent conflict between management and leadership; structure and chaos;

---

[72] After working with many managers of businesses, they universally report that their daily job is finished by about 10 am, leaving the rest of the day free for leisure or generative activities.

control and flow. As businesses establish, the managers tend to evict the leaders resulting in a stable but terminally-ill patient.[73]

Highly competitive environments instead of productive co-operative environments, as office politics and false competition divert attention from the task in hand. Co-operative teams can out-perform normal teams by over five to one in productivity and effectiveness. Networkers tend to be rewarded for their visibility rather than for their competence - the competent are mostly invisible as there are no complaints and customer praise is rare.

These factors raise stress and make us need to switch off. We make ourselves ill to get away from the draining "busy bee" syndrome, and we seek diversions. As far back as Roman times this was well known to the ruling classes and the intelligentsia. They used the concept of "bread and circuses" to keep the mob population sufficiently well fed and well entertained that they would not consider revolution.

We get hypnotised by TV and receive implanted negativity. Soaps and news programmes are focussed on the negative and drag down our spiritual vibration. Computer games and the internet occupy our minds to divert us away from our purpose.

Britain is one of the highest-taxed countries in terms of visible taxes, but also with large invisible taxes, such as in the form of commercial rental and land prices. Enforced conformity is designed into the system, for example in the law, where speed cameras are located for revenue generation rather than at schools or black spots). Insurance and institutionalised gambling (stock market) all take their share of taxing away the "money". Debt is the economic control, which is why debt is not legal in France; one has to pay off one's bills every month.

The illusion of freedom comes through the illusion of independence and material possessions. Personal isolation is increased through reduced parent-child time, competitive environments, and the break-up of communities into isolated households. We are all inter-dependent, but only have strength together. So, any manipulative power seeks to separate.

---

[73] This happens at many levels, meaning that drones predominate where a few "superstars" could do the job far better and cheaper. I saw this in action with a team of ten that could outperform a hundred, consistently and by ever-growing margins.

Education has moved from its original roots to a reductionism versus spiritual experience, passing tests rather than growing intelligence, conformity through stick not carrot, crime and punishment, uniform and levelling.

We lack a strong United Nations or other moderating authority over common resources like fish, oil, sea, wood and minerals, and so they are wasted. It seems that while we may not like dictatorships, common resources can only be preserved by a powerful regulatory force (stick), as poverty and the desire for scarce resource are the drivers for consumption. By a curious coincidence the rise of the industrial consumer society was matched by the rise of tuberculosis - known at the time as "consumption"; a signal that society missed, of course.

Compared to even fifty years ago, the modern civilised human is far more dissociated and thus fragmented. Knowledge has truly been the seed of man's destruction and loss of power. The reason Jung's collective unconscious therapy has fallen into greater disuse is because the individual psychological conditioning is so great that very few people get to experience the group mind; and they most likely get locked up.

Modern man lives the illusion of superiority, but the giants of old dwarf the modern weakling, whether it is comparing ancient Greek rowers or even the minds of the Victorian scientific greats.

Solutions from within the fragmented, social world

- One side wins: terms are imposed - how long before rebellion happens? (e.g. England-Wales-Scotland, Balkans, all empires, ...)

- Truce: separate land/territory (e.g. the Pope's accord with Portugal and Spain in the 1500's, boundaries)

- Both sides are destroyed (exhaustion ends the Athens-Sparta war)

- Sufficient pain that both side choose a new way to cooperate - a temporary peace, or longer (e.g. the EU).

- A common enemy/threat (when a train stops in tunnel the normal social barriers break down and people begin to talk and help each other, or the Second World War where a common enemy united the other nations, or see what happens in the films "Mars Attacks" and "Independence Day")

- The Great King - the "King's Peace" (Persia, old China, Japan - the Shogun, Roman Empire, one-God religions). The problem is if there are many great kings - no single Great King wins.
- The methods of power and control described above.

The conflict between state and religion first arose with Henry II and Thomas Beckett, took its correct form with Henry VIII and settled with the abdication of James II. The present problem of Sharia law and the UK state Law is a repeat of the problems addressed before. The principle of Henry VIII is that the state must be above the religion. The head of state must also be head of any other religions operating legally in this country. Their leaders must defer to the head of state or leave the country. Without this, in the UK we are in for a revisiting of the civil war and strife of the Tudor and Stuart ages, until the state is again agreed supreme over religion.

The problem with there being more than one great king is the conflict between them, the same as three one-God religions makes a crowd; one would have done. Therefore, the one-God religious solution is not viable without too great a cost in human life and destruction.

Beyond the fragmented, social world

We require natural channels for aggression and testosterone, "if a game is not working, change the rules". The vision of this world is healthy competition, like Tibetan debates or the idyll of the American sporting ethos - "as long as it's a good game". I contrast this to the cheating of the unhealthy game as shown in European soccer - diving, play-acting, intimidating referees, professional fouls and bribery or match-fixing.

The context of the visioned world is "we"; cooperation and stewardship, with laws that genuinely protect the masses from the elite. A manifesto for peace in our land would be laws aligned to the code of Ma'At, and appropriate punishments. It would be enforced by a global service dedicated to anti-corruption activities.

The problem of this world is the challenge of living in peace; getting people from conflict into one mind. The source of this world is one mind: the philosophy of Tibetan Buddhism, and the accelerating potential of the Holigral method. Seeing who people really are, seeing their role, respecting their role.

Social Reasons for Personal Change

Given that the self is ever-more structured, does one just continue with this, or does one seek to undo these structures? The answer is simple; if you are happy as you are, then continue, and if you are not, then maybe a midcourse tweak will do; and if that will not do then why not "go for it"?

So what kind of undesirable direction is one to cause awakening? A threat to one's very survival in the dream. Death is the natural awakening, and if there is a threat, or indeed actuality of "death" in a dream, mostly people awaken then.

One only has to notice what happens during a crisis - suddenly people start talking and helping each other, the barriers dissolve and there is no separation in the flow of those moments. When people truly realise they will only survive by cooperating then they will cooperate, just like in the early days of hunter-gatherers where everyone contributed their own part to the whole.

From this perspective, civilisation is the direct expression of a lack of trust in nature providing for human needs. Highly successful hunting human tribes must have over-hunted Europe and the Middle-East some five to ten thousand years ago, if not longer ago. We know this from the extinction of many species dating to those times and earlier.

From then we can infer that controlling the remaining herds became the next factor - assuring the harvest of the hunt without expending the energy of the hunt. We can then infer that some ancient innovators started storing grain for the off-season, and from this then emerged storage containers, buildings, land management and presumably some forms of protecting the herd and the grain from the nomadic tribes.

The warfare between city-states and nomads then fills the annals of earliest recorded history. We can infer the concept of "safety in numbers" and then the emergence of the effective administrator plus military defence, from which then emerged a "ruling class" of those with the military power. The protectors became the shepherds and those who fleeced the others, and this led to the need to feed the glory of the protectors through aggressive war.

Today is no different, with illegal occupations of oil-rich countries by occidental powers and a few controlling the world trade and the rapid exhaustion of our natural resources. As every ancient power collapsed under its own weight and resource exhaustion, and because the same power structures exist now, global collapse is inevitable without massive personal change upon the part of the silent majority.

The planet is in crisis now - well, not the planet but the creatures living on the planet, the plants and the mineral forms and the humans. Non-human species face extinction rates not seen for sixty-five million years, and entirely due to human activity. Humanity is out of balance, out of control, over-populating with distorted relative values as to the importance of the lives of humans compared to other species.

Humanity is clearly depleting resources faster than they can be regenerated, at an ever-accelerating rate. The only controls on human population are war, famine, pestilence and plague. Even these controls are overly mitigated by human actions to limit their effect. This just means a big crash when it happens, rather than natural cycles limiting the growth of humanity.

Unless massive individual action is taken by every passive, apathetic occidental human being, then it is already too late to prevent a global catastrophe that might threaten the very existence of ALL human beings.

Easter Island, the dodo and the successive extinction of so many species should be signals enough, but no, it seems we are pre-determinedly stupid, and only when it is too late will we take the steps and make the sacrifices required to bring humanity back into balance with Mother Nature. How many of the items listed below have you taken personal actions on?

- deforestation, soil erosion, climate change, depletion of precious metals, oil consumption
- If you have seen tropical logging first hand then the scale of devastation is fully brought home. Until you have seen whole landscapes destroyed you really do not see the works of Sauron and Saruman[74] in action in the modern world.
- illegal war and occupations, war crimes like Guantanamo Bay
- one hundred percent recycling - including human bodies; countryside protection from urbanisation
- animal sanctuaries or protection from cruelty, child abuse, anti-slavery and child/abused labour

---

[74] These are the evil warlord-wizards of J.R.R. Tolkien's Middle Earth, who destroy the forests to build the weapons of war.

- the Nestlé boycott over dried milk in Africa, GM crops and antibiotics in animals
- body care, diet and exercise
- drugs and crime in your area, community service and actions
- overpopulation, cash crops from famine areas, desertification
- over-consumption of water in overpopulated, over-grazed places like Australia, coupled with large-scale deforestation
- arms trades and conflicts, unethical politicians, government and laws biased for the rich
- spending locally, sharing your wealth, charitable activities and substantial donations
- investing in your own personal development
- looking at how you are personally creating this world, plastics versus natural products
- education provision and learning difficulties, helping the disadvantaged
- and ... widespread, massive corruption.

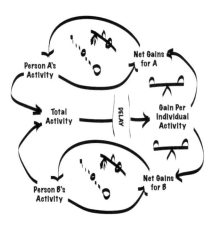

Tragedy of the Commons systems archetype (Senge]

This planet is poisoned by human activity - waste, pollution, desertification, deforestation, de-mineralisation, debunking, spiritually bankrupt, financially bankrupt and nearing resource bankruptcy. Unless we each accept total responsibility for changing this, nothing will change - it is not up to a few of us, or even a few hundred thousand. Billions of us must start to cooperate together, and only this way can the disparities and scarcity myths be redressed. To do this, enough influential people have to "wake up" and look further than the ends of their noses.

Clever boys, got loads of toys,
Nuclear den, their way then,
No air? Die then.

Wake up Joe, forests must go
Who needs air, to breathe fair
Chop chop, that's it.

Pension plan? O silly man,
Without trees, nought to ease
Burn, and cough.

Imagine life, after we've gone
Credit spent, earth bank rent,
Our children, dead.

Extinction, never so fast,
Human err, puts them past,
Cannibal Jim!

Tick tock clock, asleep forgot
Late to save, earthly grave
Act fast, oh clot.

Mother earth asleep, wake up,
Soon to weep, tidal waves,
A crust, to clean.

8.6 Thursday Conclusion

The fundamental delusion of occidental society is this; the word "individual". Yes we each have one body that cannot be divided, but this does not mean that the same applies to the mind. Contradictory programs, desires, wishes, expectations, conflicting wants and needs, and different aspects of personality reveal themselves through this one physical body.

Sometimes the programs run sequentially, sometimes in parallel. This gives a greater variety than how computers work, but runs along the same metaphorical lines of different computing architectures. Our technological and artistic creations are but mirrors of our minds. For example, some people have a mind full of parallel rapid conversations.

Flows things to complete their purpose and they die. The solutions of the Thursday problems are the Friday 'we' and the Friday 'death'.

9 Death

9.1 Friday Processes

The highest level of these intelligence systems is strategic and diplomatic, involving long-term planning, bringing a campaign to a successful conclusion for all parties involved. The physics relevant to diplomacy is that of relativity, because all world views have to be respected as being equally valid, however wrong one might feel other people are.

Einstein postulated that all frames of reference were equally valid, and that the perspective of that frame of reference was true for that frame of reference and no others. It follows that a physicist's view of human nature will be quite different to that of an artist. The combined perspectives of many give rise to a greater sense of the whole. Two kinds of Friday process are presented; "releases" which are simple ways to let go structures or attachments at the right phase of a life cycle, and "no sacrifices", a holistic "we" perspective from the top of the pyramid model.

9.2 Releasing

The very words we use act out projective energies. While the momentum work dissolves the facilitator, the transference between client and facilitator can be large, although there is no projecting if both client and facilitator are in flow.

Out of flow, the word "you" is particularly loaded with emotional projection; the placement of energy at another person. While you may not feel it most of the time, recall a situation where a teacher or parent is telling off a child, or you yourself feel "told off", and you will feel, no doubt, the emotional blast.

This happens all of the time, mostly subliminally, but as I was becoming ever-more sensitive to the energies around I found being on the receiving end of projections increasingly uncomfortable and undesirable. I was also using more NLP-type ways to get people to experience how they projected "AT" someone else, and I wanted a cleaner approach, so I was primed for a new discovery.

At the same event as the Story-Busting was invented, in September 2007, I awoke the last morning, dreaming still of a way of rapidly releasing the pronoun structures that radiate the projections. By intention, the purpose is to undo these, through the direct, "Right Understanding" of what pronouns do, and people's usage of them. The first of these were the release processes of this chapter.

The Physics level of the matrix (Sunday) is largely outside of the normal awareness, as indeed is the boundary/adaption layer (Monday). These layers are where the energies of projections apply, where "magic" happens, if you like; magic being the term for something where there is not yet a scientific understanding.

As the consciousness of the self expands, it also expands through the matrix, and this gives one a measure of control, or a beginning of a measure of control over the structures of mind. Then one can really start to accelerate the change, taking control of one's own structures.

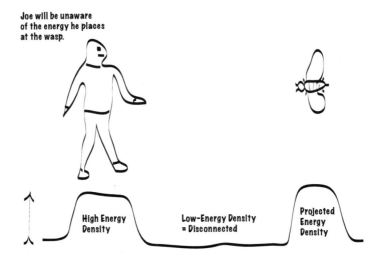

Joe will be unaware
of the energy he places
at the wasp.

High Energy
Density

Low-Energy Density
= Disconnected

Projected
Energy
Density

The **release processes** are designed to undo the projections one has applied to others, to oneself, and which one has received from others, past, present or future.

About the same time as story busting was being developed, I also created processes that were designed to consciously undo projecting, as it happens. I called them release processes, because they operated to release the "you" and "me" pronouns in relationships. They only work if a person really experientially "gets" projection; otherwise it is just words. But their power is extraordinary when used by a person who can feel the projection fields.

The keys to this process are:

   a) awareness of the power of words as spells, energetically, and

   b) understanding and kinaesthetic experience of projecting fields and emotional fields.

Without these in place, one will not feel the result, nor will the intention power suffice. As it is.

The basis of the process lies in the idea that the electrons and protons of a person's structure are their pronouns, and that the electrons are primarily "you" form, and the protons primarily "I" form.

Once two people have connected, probably emotionally at some level, they become "entangled", to use the Physics term for photons or particles having interacted. They seem to know about each other, and something done to one affects the other.

The pronouns are released because one is actually speaking to one's own "you" that is projected at the space of "the other person", not to "the other person". In this spirit, the processes are self-evident. They do not require the other person to be present; it is sufficient to name them or to bring them into your mind or awareness. The "turning away" at the end is really important.

The Mutual Release - *for use in relation to another person*

Verse 1:

I release you from being anything that I am **not**.

I release you from **not** being anything that I am.

I release you from [the tyranny of] my release.

[*optional:*

I request you to release me from being anything that you are **not**.

I request you to release me from **not** being anything that you are.

I release you from this request.]

Turn away.

Verse 2:

I release you from being [like me / who I am]

I release you from **not** being [**not** like me / who I am **not**]

I release you from [the tyranny of] this release

[*optional:*

I request you to release me from being [like you / who I am]

I request you to release me from **not** being [**not** like you / who I am **not**]

I release you from this request.]

Turn away.

Release by Issue Buster process - *for use in relation to another person:*

I meet you, you meet me, [Hello, hello.]

I release you, You release me, We release each other,

We release our life context,

We release our past [history], We release our projected future,

We choose love, acceptance and non-judgement between us,

We are one, both same and different, we are brothers [sisters].

[Turn Away.]

196

A Universal Release - *with the intention of it only applying to that which no longer serves*

> I release every single [...] from being anything I am not.
>
> I release every single [...] from not being anything I am.
>
> I release every single [...] from being released by me.
>
> I release every single [...] from being like me or from not being not like me, and I release them from this release.
>
> I offer free choice or constraint or no offer as required by every other [...].
>
> I offer myself to be that which is required, and freely offer my services or not to manifest the perfection.
>
> Or not as I feel in my as my [divine] inspiration.
>
> I commit to fully being.
>
> I also offer my refusal to play when I wish so.
>
> [Turn around, six times, slowly.]

9.3 "No Sacrifices"

There is no room for "ego" in this process, it is an entirely "we" paradigm, and the personal desires are transcended.

The physics is this: current flows from high to low voltage; it costs a huge amount of energy to force a flow the other way.

The answers to the world's problems are obvious and nothing is going to be done about them unless we do it ourselves, because it may not always serve the self-interest of those in power to do something about the real problems.

There are organisations where most people thinks someone else has the power; and not a lot of change happens in them. Risk is lowered progressively until ossification sets in. So we have to find other ways.

"We" call everything either a game or a story. This is not in a negative sense of psychological problems and the schoolyard, but rather in the positive sense that we can use the perceptual frame of "game" or "story" to better understand our focus of attention, whether its a marketplace, family life or work. Discover the game or story being played out in the life area, to understand the rules and boundaries, the roles and script.

Then think outside the box of the game, looking at a bigger game around it. By playing the bigger game one does better than staying in the smaller game.

If the game involves sacrifices then change the game - unless you are really, very, definitely sure that there needs to be a sacrifice and that there is no other way. If someone loses, change the game.

An example game change that I have used, is to apply the physics of "Watts = Volts x Amps", with the aim of making allies from potential competitors, and this involves finding out the real competition.

In tennis, the players welcomed back Justine Hennin and Kim Clijsters because, while she may have threatened other players' rankings rankings, the sport is more exciting overall. The real competition is other entertainments, not the other players. The competition for sport is "entertainment". The modern stage is the equivalent of the amphitheatre of Rome. The competition for entertainment would be other drains on household income and on people's time.

It is an old adage: *"If you cannot beat them, join them."*

Questions / Instructions	Comments ...
What is your purpose or aim?	This is the initial loading, understanding the world around.
What is happening in the world around you?	
What tactics are being displayed?	What is your role?
What roles are people taking?	A game has rules, roles and tactics.
What do their clothing and material goods reveal?	Identify the "great game" being played.
What games are being played?	
What are their boundaries and rules?	

Who else might share this aim or have a similar aim?

Who is competing with you?

What is your strength, your uniqueness?

What strengths complement yours?

Who else has these strengths?

How can these strengths work together?

Which rules can you change? and which must you leave in place?

What has been sacrificed?

Which roles can change or be adapted?

What is the dress code and-or branding?

What new tactics can you introduce?

What will then be happening?

And what will not then be happening?

How will this fulfill your purpose?

Does this fit a "we" paradigm?

Is this for the best for the world?

Hint: competitors!

Use a SWOT analysis if you wish (Strengths, Weaknesses, Opportunities, Threats)

What is your flow and or potential difference?

What is their flow and or potential difference?

Break and/or change the marketplace game and or story.

What has been gained?

What symbols might represent the work?

Or even ancient or very old tactics?

Trace this ahead 6 or more times

Are there no losers in the game/story (including minerals, plants, animals, biodiversity, ecology and people's needs).

9.4 Typical Results from a Comprehensive Use of The Method

Effects

The now-individual person will experience some or all of these effects, and more:

- The skin becomes smoother and more flexible - good collagen. Wrinkles reduce and fade, as do other facial lines - because the muscular tensions have changed, and some facial expressive habits disappear.

- Sense of smell will become more sensitive; a vegan can smell the meat or dairy that an omnivore has been consuming. Just as most people can smell the acrid urine of lions, so can sensitives tell exactly the food and chemicals that someone else has been eating. Dogs smell each other's faeces, urine and anuses to exchange information; humans swap their stories. Understanding the stories is the key to operating effectively in the matrix - hence metaphor for learning.

- Taste and diet shift - the body knows what nutrients it needs, and will guide food choice accordingly. It becomes possible to "taste" a room, to sense the people and "get" them at the taste level. Moving between countries or regions or even houses reveals different levels and cultures at all sensory levels.

- Emotions become information. They are cues as to the desired behaviour of the projections of those around, but also one has choice as to whether to act on them or not. Influencers who want to control you can become seriously frustrated when their ploys fail. Wolves should beware girls in red cloaks; the victims plays a great control game. There being zero stress, and instead an underlying calm and confidence and peace, life becomes considerably easier, with most things instantly clear and straightforward.

- Being in no-mind, thoughts are often the intruded projection of others, making mind-reading easy, and also giving further insight into people who might be trying to control a situation.

- Walking-waking meditation is the default state, with full awareness and full focus on the present activity, maximising results or allowing easy multi-tasking.

- Signals are no longer triggers from the past, they come from "here and now" or from the future, allowing one to change course and anticipate. For example, in tennis it is possible to know the opponent's shot one to two seconds before it is made. In football, predicting where a penalty shot is going to end up becomes an easy game. This energetic linking can even be driven in the other direction, choosing for the unaware opponent; not that I advocate this, nor endorse exploiting such advantages in sport, for that would destroy the wonderful, gallant, British loser.

- Other healing modalities like Reiki or energy forms, or even massage and acupressure, can become intuitive gifts that one can just know how to do with no training. Clairsentient skills can also be cultivated or grown with practice, as can divination and such arts.[75]

"All is Mind.", The Kybalion

Mind-Field

The mind-field, being the structure of the selves, rules over the emotional and body fields, and even the sense of self, and the soul rules all. The primal projection at conception is the ancestral codes carried in the DNA, and these set the starting conditioning - the "Saturday" environment that is the physical, emotional and mental bodies inherited from the parental gene pool.

Rather than the "mind" ruling, though, I would rather say that the energetic structure rules, and that there is a mind per structure, and the body has to reflect the complex set of structures being held within the person's being. Likewise, the emotional responses are automatic reflexes once the structures are in place, and choice only exists outside of having the structures.

The body reflects and takes on the consequences of the energetic attractors (Sunday level), including postural factors like a bent back under a metaphysical weight. The body is the most strongly manifested aspect of the acquired projections.

As people age, so their character becomes ever-more evident in their faces and postures, until it is fixed in fused bone groupings. I have met one

---

[75] Not everyone will be able to; it depends upon structures liberated and other factors.

person who was playing out the wicked witch of Snow White, and yes the nose and chin and upper back really do give away the identity very strongly. Another time, when visiting Barcelona, my hostess explained it was a city of pirates, and I noticed that one introduced businessman there had even sailed to the Caribbean and had an archetypal pirate face.

Psycho-Soma

I believe all illness to be psycho-somatic in cause, although deeply hidden within the unconscious; even accidents have causes due to lacks of awareness or soul-effects. As the body is the most manifest result of the acquired projections, adaptions and self-creations, it is also the biggest signal of the release of completing the work. If diseases, illnesses, and even cancers were to have a psycho-somatic cause, then the mind could also undo such illnesses. There are no medical explanations for spontaneous remissions of cancers and illnesses, so I can hypothesise (not theorise), that psycho-soma might underly such remissions.

Dress

The clothing will also represent the character, although there is more room for disguise, and I agree with Eric Berne's analysis that Little Red Riding Hood will very likely appear wearing a red coat with integral hood - having now seen this enough times. The wolf does indeed have a wonderful set of teeth and a huge grin. So, the body signals give strong, difficult-to-mask clues to the person seeking to read the story-level identity (Wednesday level) of someone else, or even of themselves.

Reducing Tensions

In summary, the results clean up the postures and relax the muscle tensions that drive the habitual gestures and postures, bringing a more upright and balanced way of physically being. It rejuvenates the body, especially noticeably the skin softening and lines reducing or disappearing, the toxins leaving the body once the associated structures have dissolved, and the energy levels increasing significantly, unnecessary weight being spontaneously lost in many cases.

Toxic Release

When the life force returns, some astounding body effects occur. First and foremost is the re-heating effect, as the life force re-integrates. This lasts anything up to a few hours, and is synonymous with the outpouring of toxins from the associated lymph nodes. The toxins flush though the skin, and the client may need several showers over a few days, and to drink a lot of water, as their body system naturally releases chemicals no longer required or held by structures. This is a key part of how addictions are released, and a key measurable evidence, before and after the work.

The corollary of this detoxifying effect is that sweat lodges and saunas only offer temporary fixes for the toxins, as they will re-accumulate in the lymphs associated with the structures that attract them. Only freeing the metaphysical structures will give a permanent release.

Flexibility

The second body effect is a renewed flexibility. We have had seventy-year-olds sitting on the floor like a toddler, bendy as a real youngster; with no effort and no body exercises. My theory is that the mind holds the body tensions. An unconscious body is highly flexible, and therefore it has to be the mind structures that create stiffnesses and the like. The net effect is more flexibility, grace, smooth movement, a reduction in injuries and reduced bruise healing times. Two people with injured knees have reported i) returning to skiing with no side-effects, ii) a complete absence of any limp.

The third body effect is the skin. It becomes softer, more flexible, younger, more reflexive, better toned and it looks younger; many years younger.

The Body Signals

The posture, facial features, gestures, clothing, hair, expressions, muscle tensions, typical aches and pains, bodily weaknesses and internal organ dispositions all indicate strong signals as to the structures of the self that the client has. These are augmented by figures of speech and turns of phrase, but the body language really does contribute significantly to the detective work of the facilitator and client working as a team for the healing of the client.

That the body takes on the posture of a character in a story, including things like growing a bony chin or hooked nose, shows that the body manifests the personal structures. I remember my daughter being able to manifest an illness within minutes of being informed of some activity she did not want to do, even from a very young age. This first clued me into the underlying nature of illness as psycho-somatic. However, it is all deeply unconscious, and it is not fair to blame a person for being ill when they have no control over their structures, especially as sickness is really the only socially acceptable excuse for some down-time from work, given the stresses and pressures of modern life. I recall a director of one business who would always be off sick with a bad back during the most stressful times; convenient but also necessary for survival.

What the body shows is the most materialised structures, and so they are the toughest ones to work out. It might take some time for the body to recover, and in advanced conditions, it might be the case that damage to bones or joints or body organs mean that the body signals cannot be fully undone; what has been manifested has been manifested. The earlier we can catch and heal a signal, the more completely its effects can be dissolved and the body appear as if it never was.

Nonetheless, some signals are body only, and it makes sense to work directly with signals that seems to have little or no mind-field associated.

Working the body directly

Over the years of running emergent experiences, I have developed a wide range of ways of enabling emergence to happen naturally. One of the most important, primal aspects is the body signals, whether chemical, muscular, emotional, skeletal or functional in nature.

As an augmented practice to the mind-emotion work of Holigral, I have tried the Bowen Method, the Feldenkrais Method, Reiki, massage, shamanic massage, lymphatic drainage, acupuncture, kinesiology and reflexology. My present conclusion is that the most effective combination for ensuring the body signals are acknowledged, respected and supported in doing their job is Feldenkrais, combined with saunas and our own form of body-touch.

The body-touch is a gentle finger-point at wherever feels right. Emotions or memories are released, revelations happen, and then another point may be touched. Unlike acupressure, which follows patterns of meridians, there is no systemic model, but a few simple touch-and-hold actions have, for example, released a frozen shoulder and neck with no recurrence of the symptoms.

I find that completing the Holigral approach leads to the body naturally detoxifying. This is as if the toxins held are markers of the key events and phases in life. By doing the bodywork, specifically, the client can also release the signals only held bodily; these are without obvious mind / linguistic / verbal /emotional signals.

The Awareness Effect

The awareness benefits depend on one's starting awareness, so many people will have many of these already, but it makes sense for me to start from my perception of "a normally dissociated and socialised person". They include:

- becoming aware of "the real other side" - the deeper layers of the pyramid model - ancestors, spirits, entities, angels, Gods and so forth; potentially clairsentience or mediumship,

- becoming aware of the group mind; dreams may shift into the more Jungian forms,

- fully associated emotional experience and insight, sensitivity of others, feeling precise emotions and knowing who they come from, maybe even to the levels of a medical intuitive, in any of physical, emotional and mental pains of others; maybe synaesthesias involving the perception of auras (the illusions of the astral realm),

- archetype awareness; seeing the archetypes in other people,

- resilience to hypnosis; one remains in a state others might call a deep hypnosis, but highly functional; one is a walking meditation, and such practices are no longer required,

- others may be attracted by the now shiny self - this can have a downside (think lights and moths),

- inner peace, and understanding Tibet and its group mind-field,

- seeing and meeting people, on the level; no-mind in everyday life

- for autistics, this might bring association into the social matrix, and understanding of the social codes and energies happening at the tribal level, which otherwise will appear mysterious and full of complex, impenetrable rules, for nonlexics this might bring understanding and ability to structure like the lexics, and for lexics this might bring the experience of the full mind-experience of the nonlexics; liberation.

"There is always something going on." Hot Fuzz

The first emergent awareness is that of understanding signals; realising, recognising, hearing, seeing, feeling and accepting the gatekeepers of personal transformation within, and also the reading of signals in the world around. The clues are so widespread that reading people rapidly becomes a personal Sherlock-Holmes kind of skill.

Because one has had one's own signals repetitively drawn to one's attention, one starts to see the signals in everything happening. This is just like seeing everywhere the same kind of car that one has recently bought. The awareness is more sensitive to the signs, omens and portents in daily life.

The more complete the wholeness that has resulted, the more completely psychoactive life is. The more psychoactive life is, the more effortless and flowing it becomes. Then one is working with and flowing with the matrix rather than fighting it, and so one's energy is conserved, and more can be achieved.

The second emergent awareness is the clarity of peace of mind. With only one focus at a time, with one's whole attention, each "problem" in life is easily and quickly addressed. And if a problem does persist, it is a signal and readily processed using the methods learnt.

Typical business results are a reduction of working hours from a long day to maybe needing only one or two hours. This comes from clarity, rapid decisions, an absence of procrastinating and an absence of wasting time with low probability opportunities or low interest topics.

The third emergent awareness is the sense of association-dissociation in relation to present happenings. The key signal is the presence of either peace or a stressor emotion. The peace itself feels like a velvety smooth weightless yet grounded ease and comfort, but is beyond any of these words' ability to convey; it's just the best feeling. Some people may have experienced something like this in post-coital bliss. If you have, then imagine life lived like that. The stressor emotion is a signal of a happening in the world around; kind of an early-warning signal to notice something going on.

9.5 The Friday conclusion

There should be nothing left to say - peace is the only answer ... RIP

10 The Cycle

10.1 Introducing "Saturday" Processes

It may seem odd to conclude with the first day of the week, but as this represents the whole cycle, it can be better understood having first explored the other days.

The requirements phase of a project includes all the assumptions, inherited and environmental considerations and legacies from past cycles. It is a smart idea to audit the entire cycle to determine the actual origin and therefore the best kind of intervention, if there is to be one.

As Saturday is also the form of relating and relationship, the first process selected to represent this form is called "seven aspects of relating".

10.2 Seven Aspects of Relating (cycle)

Relating is dynamic, involving the whole being, both object-oriented and flow-momentum in form. Communicating has a kind of primal hierarchy relating to the sequence of ages of learning representing a kind of pyramidal structure of overlaid forms.

At the most primal, we have the chemical and emotional environment of the foetus. The baby is gaze-oriented and touch-taste-grasping. The gaze is totally face-focussed, implying that facial gestures are the next most powerful layer of communicating. Nonverbal sounds then follow, together with gestural habits.

Every single expression, muscular twitch, nonverbal um or click or err, yes or hmm, has multiple meanings depending upon context, just like every letter and every word has a different contextual meaning. This applies at every level; there is a new context and new connotations.

From words, we go to sentences, and integrated communications of emotion, body-face-gesture. The higher levels of complexity become more abstract, with hidden meaning, metaphor and symbols acquiring their places. And these subordinate into social fields and patterns.

Relating is not just to people, it is to objects, subjects and topics, jobs, hobbies, and more. The model looks at a relationship using a life-cycle, that works for businesses, products, jobs, schooling and relationships. The model assumes that everything is a phase that one passes through. By understanding how one relates in each phase, one gains flexibility of choice to be different in new relationships. The seven phases are:

- requiring - requirements: what people want from a relationship
- conditioning - initial responses: how the initial interaction goes
- adapting - assessment: how we adapt and change in response
- developing - development: how the relationship develops over time
- polishing - manufacture: how the relationship is fine-tuned to serve both parties
- serving - in-service: how the relationship serves those involved
- retiring - retirement: how we close / dispose and retire a relationship

Chaos Theory rules in nature. The small starting conditions give rise to what follows. Therefore it is important to understand especially well the early phases of a relationship for clues to what then will happen.

Question / Instruction	Comment
Choose a person with whom you had a relationship, in the past.	Or a subject. The purpose is to begin understanding the lifecycle of your relationships.
What did I want from this relationship before it started? What did they want from this relationship before it started? What were your needs?	*Requiring* Overall, general question, introducing. [me, another person, a subject, an object] [e.g. emotionally / mentally / spiritually / physically / sexually / security / communication]

As they become aware of me, how are they relating to me, as they become aware of me?

As I become aware of them, how am I relating to them, as I become aware of them?

Conditioning

Given a new requirement, one encounters new problems. How you deal with these is part of your cycle. If you need to upgrade this life aspect then choose another process for that task and then continue this process.

Then what happens?

And as that is happening, what is happening as that is happening?

Adapting

Ask this couplet of questions a few times to see how the interactions develop.

These can reveal how you find solutions to your problems, and also whether these are the best solutions.

As time goes by, how do they change how they relate to me?

As time goes by, how do I change how I relate to them?

How else do I/they change, as time goes by?

Developing

Having understood the requirements, problems and solutions, you can move beyond these through learning and insight. How well does this part of your cycle work?

Ask this question a few times.

What did they do to fine-tune this relationship?

What did I do to fine-tune this relationship?

How did it stabilise into the form that lasted longest?

Polishing

Ask these questions a few time. Fine-tuning can include making things worse.

How have they been serving me through this relationship?

What was I getting from this relationship?

How was I serving them through this relationship?

What were they getting from it?

What did you each do or not do to keep it working or to improve it?

What changes did they want?

What changes did you want?

What do they do, or not do, that contributes to ending the relationship?

What do I do, or not do, that contributes to ending the relationship?

What kind of relationship was this?

Is there anything incomplete about this relationship?

Serving

The more enduring part of a relationship is this phase, when it is in full flow, in service. While it might need maintaining, it is the consequence of the developing phases that went before.

The area of improvement here is how you maintain relationships once their pattern is established.

Also, mid-life upgrades and maintenance apply in this phase.

Retiring

All relationships will at some point end once there is no longer the common ground or mutual interests that keep it going; even if just because one of the parties dies. Ending relationships cleanly is also an art form.

When the requirements are no longer being met, a relationship is going to decline; this is natural.

What have I got from this
relationship?
What have they got from it?
Now review the pattern of this
relationship.

Going back over this relationship:
What did you really want, at the
beginning?
Did you get it?
What did you assume, but not state
or ask for, at the beginning?
What affected you most?
In response, how did you change?
How did you develop or grow?
What did you learn?
What did it stabilise into?
How did it serve you?
What changes did they want?
What changes did you want?
How did it end?

Now choose a person who is
presently in your life.
Use the above questions to find out
where you are in the lifecycle of this
relationship.
What, if anything, would you like to
do differently, in this relationship?
What do you know about yourself
now?

Review Phase (outside of the cycle)

A Wider Review
Now review what you know about
how more of your relationships have
cycled.
Think back on other relationships
and on those ongoing now.
Give them a health check using this
process.
Check the masculine, the feminine
and the ancestral aspects. Does any
of your relating reflect your parents'
relationships? If so, how?

The next relationship.

Check Your Requirements!
Use one of the other processes to
address any problem or issue
relating to what you would like to be
different - until things as are you
wish. Or, "pull back" the stage to its
beginning and rehearse a new
pattern for the stage.

Transcripts

[BEGINNING OF TRANSCRIPT]

Choose a person with whom you had a relationship, in the past.

Okay, I choose <name>.

What did I want from this relationship before it started?

This was a personal relationship, I wanted sex, companionship, fun, and a possible mate for life.

What did they want from this relationship before it started?

I can only think - I do not know. I think they wanted me, we were both attracted to each other. I felt a strong sexual connection. This was on offer.

As they become aware of me, how are they relating to me, as they become aware of me?

Eye contact, lots of eye contact, they showed me an open body, legs apart, inviting. Tension, definitely lots of tension, the tension of desire.

As I become aware of them, how am I relating to them, as I become aware of them?

I was thinking how to get them on their own, to be together without other people around.

Then what happens?

We managed that, and we developed a relationship from there.

and as that is happening, what is happening as that is happening?

We saw more of each other, and made plans.

Then what happens?

We followed through with the plans, and were very happy for a long time.

and as that is happening, what is happening as that is happening?

I think we started to develop a number of new, common interests, which kept the relationship doing new things together.

Then what happens?

I started to sacrifice my interests from before for the sake of the common, new ones.

and as that is happening, what is happening as that is happening?

I definitely missed my *****, which I loved, it was my passion from childhood, and I was spending less time on this. But this happened over a long time, you know, like it took nearly 10 years before I stopped playing it.

Then what happens?

Then other things took over, gardening and things related to the house. While they were enjoyable, they were not passionate.

and as that is happening, what is happening as that is happening?

Then the house interior design started to change, not so much as my taste but theirs.

Then what happens?

I did not think about this at the time, but I started to spend more time at work. I even went in on Saturdays to do some study for course work.

and as that is happening, what is happening as that is happening?

I started to become uncomfortable at home. The garden became my home more than the house.

Then what happens?

I developed a new interest that we did not share.

and as that is happening, what is happening as that is happening?

I think that was the beginning of the end.

As time goes by, how do they change how they relate to me?

We both became busier people at work, and with things to do at home. We became more distant, and really we only connected more deeply on holiday. This might be a usual pattern for people?

As time goes by, how do I change how I relate to them?

I become more distant, I check on them less, I spend more time connecting to other people.

How else do I/they change, as time goes by?

I'm getting the feeling this is my fault. Am I the one who takes the blame? We become more distant, I start to feel criticised. Am I inviting this?

How else do I/they change, as time goes by?

I do feel like I'm disempowered, somehow they have taken power and I am feeling like I cannot speak out, like I have to stay silent on my perspective.

How else do I/they change, as time goes by?

If I am not speaking out then this is going to be a growing problem, probably I start to resent and feel constrained.

How else do I/they change, as time goes by?

I guess I break the constraints by avoiding, by making life outside of the relationship.

How else do I/they change, as time goes by?

They want to provoke a reaction. That must be because I am not reacting, so things get worse. They speak out more and I speak out less.

How else do I/they change, as time goes by?

Bloody hell, my father never spoke out, and this must be his pattern, at least in part. And my mother would have a real go at him. This is their story, not mine, but mine also now.

What did they do to fine-tune this relationship?

Oh they had the same damned cycles, of working, distancing, finding other things to stay away, and separating from a common life. Jeeee-sussss. And arguments.

What did I do to fine-tune this relationship?

I played my father. **** this for a game of soldiers. I'm not playing this one any more. There has to be another way.

How have they been serving me through this relationship?

They played my mother, as she was with my father. Different, but the pattern was the same. This time, though, I left, not she.

What was I getting from this relationship?

I was getting to know what I did not want. I recognised that next time was going to be different, we were going to stay connected, speak and keep everything clear.

How was I serving them through this relationship?

I think her father never spoke out to her mother, so we played out a variation of her parenting. We did make a massive difference in how we parented though.

What were they getting from it?

I think they were getting something much better than they had grown up, but definitely I was becoming not what they had bargained for in the beginning. I changed and that broke the relationship. It was really my fault. I believe that.

What do they do, or not do, that contributes to ending the relationship?

Criticise me, tell me they are better off when I am not at home.

What do I do, or not do, that contributes to ending the relationship?

Oh, that is easy, I started to have affairs. I basically went out to find a replacement relationship. That sounds bad, I had tried therapy a few years earlier and I really did try to change myself, and I think the accommodation was too great.

What kind of relationship was this?

An affair, a companionship for a long while. I can look back with enjoyment of the vast majority of it.

Is there anything incomplete about this relationship?

Probably we have not said everything we could have. I do not think this is something I have control over. For now I would be happy to be friendly, but distant is as it has to be.

What have I got from this relationship?

A decision to never make the same mistakes again, to keep relationships open at all times, to make sure any distance is immediately addressed - shadows also.

What have they got from it?

The children, and I hate to say it, but a kick in the teeth, that is undeserved and unfair.

Now review the pattern of this relationship.

It started from the conditions that we both wanted, but I changed, and she did not change with me. I take full responsibility, and I accept the blame for its failure, for my part.

Now review what you know about how your relationships have cycled.

I decided after that, that I would not be the one ending relationships. I think all I did was then to create the conditions where the other person would leave. That is not so healthy, either.

There is an attraction, and a honeymoon period, then if it stays clear things go well, but if things are left unsaid the relationship becomes rocky. I've learnt therefore to try to address these things as they happen, but not everyone is up for doing this, and I'm not going to take the blame.

What did you really want?

Sex and company.

Did you get it?

Not as I wanted.

What affected you most?

Criticism.

How did you change?

I withdrew and I went out to be in nicer places.

How did you develop or grow?

I developed myself, with the aim of making the relationship work.

What did you learn?

Keep it fresh and clear. Make sure we both are getting what we want. Maintain it.

How did it serve you?

I learned a lot about myself. I am a better person for it, even if I behaved very badly.

How did it end?

Badly. I really must do something about ending relationships in a better way.

Now choose a person who is presently in your life.

Okay, I have them in mind.

Use the above questions to find out where you are in the lifecycle of this relationship.

We have kept our time together fun. We spend a lot of time together, we still really like each other's company. Yes I have many outside interests but I drop them in preference to be with my partner. I have created work that takes me away, but it is controlled and plans are to reduce this now, and to get more time at home. This is actually the most I've ever been at home.

Where is it in the cycle? It is in service. It is pretty healthy. I'm being asked to engage in some home projects, I notice this, could it be a pattern of not feeling at home? No, I am involved, I initiated the changes to home structure, and we are definitely working together.

I think we are entering a period now of maintenance, keeping stable something that is working well, and I hope happily ever after!

What, if anything, would you like to do differently, in this relationship?

Right. Now that I see my old patterns, I'm going to watch for any signals of repeating. Anything at all and I'm on it.

[END OF TRANSCRIPT 1]

The client has plenty of things they could address with 'holigral 1' processes as a result of the exercise. The process can be then used to health-check other present relationships and to change the patterns at play.

[Transcript 2]

Choose a person with whom you had a relationship, in the past.

It was a girl I knew in school, my best friend by the time I left.

What did I want from this relationship before it started?

Nothing really, we didn't intentionally start it. We were all members of the same group of girls that used to hang round together. We each had our particular friends within that group, and sometimes we all used to get together, like at breaktimes or in PE

What did they want from this relationship before it started?

I can't imagine that they wanted anything, except perhaps another friend.

[Comment: There was no innate attraction.]

As they become aware of me, how are they relating to me, as they become aware of me?

Well, we were all friendly to each other, but not overly so. I don't think, to start with, that we had a lot in common except for the friends that we both knew.

As I become aware of them, how am I relating to them, as I become aware of them?

I enjoyed being friends with her, and I would chat when the opportunity arose, but I would not actively seek her out to spend time with her, and we did not socialise outside school.

Then what happens?

Time passes. The friendships within the group ebb and flow, with some people dropping out and others joining. I did not stay friends with most of the group for the two years leading up to O levels, I had a different friend in particular with whom I preferred to spend my time. Then a number of people left school at 16, and the remaining people in the 6th form had to remake their friendships for the time they were doing their A levels.

and as that is happening, what is happening as that is happening?

Unlikely people start spending a lot of time in one another's company. Lots of us discover that we have more in common than we first realised.

As time goes by, how do they change how they relate to me?

We find a mutual enjoyment of drinking too much cider, and find that we enjoy one another's company. Also, we are in the same English class, and she often depends on me to prop her up through the bits that she doesn't understand.

As time goes by, how do I change how I relate to them?

I enjoy her company more and more, and she introduces me to people and activities and concepts that I would not have met in my 'other' world.

How else do I/they change, as time goes by?

I become much more relaxed and find it much easier to be with a wider group of people and make more friends, or at least friendly acquaintances.

What did they do to fine-tune this relationship?

Provide a venue (her home, very close to school) for our drinking sessions and for us to hang out when school had finished. Keep arranging for a whole bunch of us to go out places in the evenings and at weekends, so I was included in that.

What did I do to fine-tune this relationship?

I have no idea. Looking back, it feels like I just went along for the ride, but at the time we were simply enjoying being teenagers with no responsibility and with lots of time on our hands to have a laugh. I guess also I provided her with a stable friendship in school, when all the rest of her friends had left at 16.

How have they been serving me through this relationship?

She helped me to understand and discover that I was not doomed to be the repressed little mouse that I was becoming in my home environment. She lived in a world of fashion and make-up and boys and cars and drinking and fun, which was about as far from my home life as it could possibly be.

What was I getting from this relationship?

I became part of a very enjoyable group of friends, and had a wonderful time doing it. Looking back, it was the most fun I had anywhere at all until one brief time in my 20's, and then from my mid-30's onwards.

How was I serving them through this relationship?

I was providing her with a 'partner in crime' when we were having an illicit drink (even in school, we would keep a bottle of cider in her locker, and it was a huge laugh to try and sneak off and have a few swigs when we shouldn't). I was supporting her and helping her through her most academic A level, which she found difficult.

What were they getting from it?

A new bunch of friends for the two years of the A levels. Help with the English course. Someone who she could teach things to (like make-up), so she will have felt superior when academically she wasn't.

What do they do, or not do, that contributes to ending the relationship?

We had been collaborating on writing a book, a children's story, and a combination of events in my life (including getting divorced, which was a major upheaval), meant that I could not give the project the time and attention that she wanted to put into it. She got more and more frustrated with the lack of progress, and eventually wrote to me to say that she was going to continue with it on her own, and she couldn't work with me any more.

What do I do, or not do, that contributes to ending the relationship?

The relationship ended about 20 years after we left school. For years we had been meeting up sporadically, and chatting on the phone occasionally, but I was finding that most often we were just rehashing stories from our school days, and there was very little that we would talk about regarding our lives that we had made since then. They were too separate.

Also, she started organising a yearly event at her house, where she would invite lots of friends over for the weekend and they would spend the entire time getting as drunk as possible. She started this just after my first child was born, and although at that time I would have enjoyed it, I could not go because of the baby. I was already suffering from sleep deprivation, and I was breastfeeding, so staying up all night for two nights and consuming large amounts of alcohol were out of the question. As the years passed, I still never managed to make it to one of these events, because of the arrival of another baby and difficulties in organising childcare for a whole weekend. I even missed her wedding, which she sprung on everyone as a surprise event at one of these weekend binges.

The problem with the writing collaboration began part way through it, when we had done all the bits that were going to flow out easily, and were on the hard graft of filling in the gaps and re-writing the existing material to make it read more fluently. I was given a copy of a computer game, which I found utterly addictive and absorbing, and it began to take the place of the writing when I had free time to spend. This slowed progress to a crawl, and was probably the start of her frustration.

After that, I had a series of things happen in my life which absorbed a huge amount of my time and energy, and I lost momentum with the writing. I always kept it there in the background, like a kind of comfort blanket, but I never worked on it enough to satisfy what she wanted. At that time, she was writing for 6 hours a day at least, and often more, and did not understand why I could not do the same.

What kind of relationship was this?

Really, it was a friendship of convenience at the start. We had very little in common apart from drinking and English lessons, and when they were taken away, we simply had very little in common.

[Comment: The problem was there before the relationship existed.]

Is there anything incomplete about this relationship?

I was very upset about what happened when she told me that she did not want to work with me on the writing, because I was going too slowly for her. It felt like she had torn away my cushion - the writing had been there for years, and was my safety net, in a way. I knew her reasons for the choice she made, and I know that I was mostly responsible for it, but I still felt completely betrayed by her.

What have I got from this relationship?

An understanding that I can write children's stories if I put my mind to it. A better understanding of the writing process, which has helped me immensely in other aspects of my life since. Someone, when I was in school, who enjoyed my company and who helped me to understand that I could be the person that I wanted to be, not just the one that other people expected me to be.

What have they got from it?

The confidence to go ahead and write on her own, without me propping her up.

Now review the pattern of this relationship.

It started gently, became very intense for a while, not much in common really but we made the most of what we had. Once we moved away from the things in common (school), we moved apart and developed our own separate existences. We revisited one of those aspects for a while in going back to the writing, but I needed other things to occupy me and that wasn't satisfying whatever it was that I was needing. I am something of an addictive personality, and I can move from one 'phase' to another quite abruptly, abandoning any interest in the former one because it has served its purpose for me.

Now review what you know about how your relationships have cycled.

Looking at it, this has happened several times in the past, though not many of my relationships have gone on for as long as that one, or have been as intense. I am friends with someone, or lovers, or whatever, and we both have a need that the other one fulfills in the short term. Once that need is fulfilled, or once I realise that it is not going to be fulfilled no matter how hard I try, I lose interest and move on to somewhere else.

Going back over your relationship:

What did you really want?

Companionship in school.

Did you get it?

Yes, though the whole friendship seemed to be stuck in that era - we found it very difficult to leave it behind and move on, away from the getting drunk and reminiscing.

What affected you most?

How sad I felt when it was ended.

How did you change?

I came out of my shell in school, and found that I could make friends with people just by being myself, without offering them anything except the pleasure of my company. That sounds odd, but it relates to the time before when people seemed to want to be with me only to help them with something.

How did you develop or grow?

I became much more sure of myself than I had been. I also went through a bit of a rebellious phase, and this was encouraged and sometimes facilitated by my friend. It was really good for me.

What did you learn?

How to have a laugh. How to move in new circles than the ones I had previously been used to.

How did it serve you?

It opened a really big door for me. Without that, I would have always felt that life was passing me by. Without it, I could see other people having a good time, like looking through a glass wall, but I had no way of accessing that world, the world of normal teenagers just being themselves.

What changes did they want?

-

What changes did you want?

-

How did it end?

In a way, it ended when we left school, though it took another 20 years for it to finally officially come to a close. Whenever I think of that friendship, it always and only centres around school days, and there is nothing for me in it after that.

Now choose a person who is presently in your life.

A friend who has a son the same age as my daughter.

Use the above questions to find out where you are in the lifecycle of this relationship.

Comparing this to the others, there are some significant differences, and there are some similarities.

This one also started off gently, and was a friendship of convenience from one perspective, although from another we have a considerable amount in common and I could say that circumstances brought us into one another's orbits and revealed this. We went through a time of seeing each other regularly, and a while where in both our lives there was so much happening that other interests took over and we saw one another much less often. Currently, we are in closer contact again, partly because both our children have left the mainstream schooling system and we have a lot to talk about once more.

What, if anything, would you like to do differently, in this relationship?

This time, I do not want anything from this relationship apart from friendship, and I do not expect anything in return. I do not want either of us to feel that we are imposing on the other in any way, or that we are asking for something which causes the other to have to deviate from what they want to be doing. The most important thing is that I must make the effort too, I will not just go along for the ride and let the other person do all the arranging, and make all the calls.

What do you know about yourself now?

I need to keep my friendships separate from my interests. When I look at my interests, I see that I focus on one thing for a while, to the exclusion of everything else, and then when that is done I drop it and move on to something else. If the friendship is part of that, there is a grave danger that it will be dropped or otherwise damaged by the process of moving from one thing to another.

I want my friendships to be gentle things, not too intense and not too demanding of my time, and independent of other events in my life.

[END OF TRANSCRIPT 2]

Sometimes the "missing piece of the puzzle" is outside of the cycle: it lies before the requirements and after the death of the last relationship. Sometimes a person develops a new relationship before the end of their last one; the relative phase and timing will be an important signature. After the starting conditions are set, either consciously or unconsciously, the patterns are set and resulting phases are inevitable.

If one wants to get the next relationship perfect, then it pays to put supreme attention to the start and every single developing set until it stabilises as required. To change it, a couple would have to go back to the beginning, at least through a process, preferably together, and watch for any patterns re-emerging, and kill them while they are small.

Relationships must be maintained; they require upgrades, the rules will change, the needs will change, the priorities will change. How one responds to this is going to define what happens next. If the culture is "fire the CEO when it's not working" then the people will have many divorces, because they will fire the partner rather than work it through.

226

10.3 The Personal Situation - Dreamers

Ultimately, Osiris and the Scarab beetle show all that is needed to know.

At night, how does a person realise they are dreaming? By becoming self-aware of their true identity during the dream - of their body and physicality. So too, by becoming aware of who they really are, a person begins to awaken to their real identity: "I am that which I am".

How else does a person awaken? By their consciousness emerging, spreading their identity and holding patterns of energy throughout their body. An unconscious body is limp and fully flexible - stiffness is the result of the mental body's structures.

How else does a person awaken? By being woken up - an upsetting and disruptive process, that is best avoided unless the awakener is prepared for the consequences and the emergency is considered sufficiently important to interrupt the dream.

How else does a person awaken? In a moment of inspiration or sudden illumination. How else does a person awaken? By recognising the signs, omens and portents for what they are - maybe by using meditative processes, or through performing Zen tasks, or by attaining the right understanding of enough of the environment.

How else does a person awaken? A visitor enters their dream and offers and provides the awakening, like in the film "The Matrix".

How else? Maybe they do not need to awaken.

Why would anyone require to awaken? For just a few to make a correction to the matrix, and then depart accordingly, leaving behind myths of visitations of the Gods or Prophets.

Why else? Because the programming had failed? Not possible; because of who the programmer is.

Why else? To live lucidly, because it is time to take control and correct the course of a dream that is heading in an undesirable direction.

Why else? Nope, that is it!

A Maze

How did it come to this?

Every way out just leads back in.

What kind of maze has no escape?

Why, one tailor made for a mind.

How does a person undo such a maze?

Whatever you do, it changes the rules.

Who made the maze, unmake it can.

But, where to find the architect?

Why, try a mirror and go deeper and deeper.

And what's inside?

Layer on layer: six dimensions of space and six of time.

Traverse these spaces to find the grail.

What secret does it bear?

The grail knows this: "The Land and the King are One."

Understand these words and free you can be.

A new life: both in and out.

Both free and a player, embodied creator alive.

11 The Afterlife

11.1 Processes Beyond the Cycle

The days of the week address "when, why, what, where, who, how and the effect". The frame of the observer is the eighth factor. The ancestral, cultural and group-mind factors are addressed using the types of processes already covered within the cycle. The example given here addresses ancestral factors.

11.2 Clean Ancestors

Lifelong problems/habits/goals/issues/concerns/needs/desires, or those which you have had for a long time, may well have intergenerational patterns. One way of therefore escaping a karmic chain going over many generations, is to use space with time, in this case the time of generations.

Ancestors, or one's projection of them, have insight into what is happening now. Very often they are the cause or a link in the chain of something we have to deal with in this life now. Cultural and ancestral patterns can have very, very long, deep roots. One example: I am fairly heretical - in the 1550's the Saunders clan was being burned at the stake - for heresy. So what had changed in that time? Just how the establishment does its burning.

The way to recognise a pattern that goes ancestral is often by omission. There may be no starting point, in this life, that can be found; something is present throughout. However, this can still be cultural, so we need more cues. If it is not ancestral, your ancestors will not have much to say on the subject. Choose another process.

Sometimes a pattern becomes evident after a certain age, because ancestrally this age has importance. If the concern does not fit any one phase of the life-cycle of phases (needs, problems, solutions, outcomes, fine-tuning, maintenance or retirement), and does not lie between two phases, then it lies between retirement and the requirements of a new phase of life.

The process uses the idea of psychological space to map out different knowings spatially, choosing those spaces that represent individuals in your ancestry.

Questions and Instructions	Comments
Find a place to be, and mark this as your space. Represent the problem here.	"Your space". Maybe write the problem on a post-it, together with your name.
Notice where your [father/mother] is. Place a post-it to mark their position. What does your [...] know about this problem? Now do the same for your other parent.	[father or mother, then the other.] Go to that position, and stay there while you answer the question.
Notice where your father's father is ... Place a post-it to mark his position. What does he know about this problem? Now do the same for your mother's mother. ... and so on, for seven generations.	Repeat this unto the seventh generation from yourself male-male and female-female. "and notice where [his father / her mother] is?" OR "and, his father, you notice, is where?" and go to that space.
And what do I know now? and now what can happen? and as [that is happening], now what is happening, as [that is happening]?	From the seventh generation back to the present; you.

Move to the next generation towards the present.

And what do I know now?

and now what can happen?

and as [that is happening], now what is happening, as [that is happening]?

Repeat until returned to "your space".

Do this for both male and female.

Transcript

[BEGINNING OF TRANSCRIPT]

Find a place to be, and mark this as your space.

Represent the problem here.

Water flowing, breakdown of 'applyancies'.

[Spelt as the client wrote the words.]

1. Notice where your mother is.

Place a post-it to mark her position. Go there.

What does your mother know about this problem?

you should have listened to me ... don't trust men ... they're all the same ... useless ... want something doing fix it yourself ... that's another disappointment ... you're just not good enough ...

2. Notice where her mother is, place a post-it to mark her position.

She's on my back, on the kidneys.

So what does she know about this?

Struggling, holding on, you're not good enough - to my mother, it's all your fault, lying little bitch, i can't trust you, you made my life hell, I'm angry with the world... something around my father having to sign for her to have a mortgage ... it was important for her to have her own house ... you have to present yourself properly to the world. nothink's fair. resentment.

3. Notice where her mother is. Place a post-it to mark her position.

On the compost bin.

231

So go there. And what does she know about this?

Gran's getting wound up about nothing, she's just highly strung. You should think yourself lucky you've got enough food to eat. You should be happy. And you brought troubles on yourself. You've made your bed and now you've got to lie in it. You have to support yourself. <name> is your responsibility. Accept what is.

4. Notice where her mother is. Place a post-it, and go there. And what does she know about this?

[Big cold air flow.] A flow river under the house. Draining energy. Move somewhere else. Water will always find a way through unless you unblock the blockage. You know what that is. Shifting earth. Worms. Composting. Rubbish. Into something good. Can flow. More energy. And nourishment. That's it.

5. Notice where her mother is. Place a post-it, and go there. And what does she know about this?

The willow tree has the answers. Bending instead of resisting. Rosemary cleansing. Keep warm. What does your heart want n know? Insecurity. Living on the streets. Put in a workhouse. Hungry. Fear. Wretched life. Want to be dead. Too many children. Such a drain. Can't cope. You have it easy. Silly girl. That's it.

6. Notice where her mother is. Place a post-it, and go there. And what does she know about this?

Cold cold hard happy. Stone. Cornwall. Wind, wind, and sea spray, cliffs, pigs. As you sow so you shall reap, planting seeds sunflowers, need to be practical. It's man's work, fixing drains or sweeping chimneys. She had an affair with the chimney sweep. Stained her black. Guilt. Pirates. That's it.

Notice where her mother is. Place a post-it, and go there. And what does she know about this?

That you need to go fishing for food. And its dangerous. Struggling to survive. A husband that died in a fishing accident. Hooks. Through worms. Little things to catch a shark. Just letting the shark go. It has a right to live. Coloured snails. Rough stone. Bare feet on rough stone. Be careful where you walk. Don't step on the snails. Munching lettuce. Seagulls, seagull rather, seagull, a different perspective. Look at the whole picture. And the answer you will know.

[And what do I know now?]

This house is too big, too much responsibility, weighing you down. Find someone to share it. Responsibility everywhere you go. You need money to survive. It's the worry weighing me down. Find a job. Part time. Cleanse the house. You need a holiday. Take care of your dog. Bones are buried in the ground. Grief weighing you down. Attaching you to this place. Anchored. With the sea can't breathe. Trapped in a tube, glass tube. You need to swim down to come up. Don't fight the water. I want to get back to Spain. I miss my family. Having to struggle all alone to survive. That's it.

And now what can happen?

I can ask for help.

And as asking for help, now what is happening, as asking for help?

less to do myself, shared responsibility.

Move to the next generation towards the present. and now what can happen?

I can eat plenty of fish.

And as you can plenty of fish, now what is happening, as you can eat plenty of fish?

Makes me feel sick.

Move to the next generation towards the present. and now what can happen?

Get rid of what I don't want.

And as getting rid of what you don't want, now what is happening, as getting rid of what you don't want?

A little bit lighter. and flowing more easy.

Move to the next generation towards the present. and now what can happen?

Flowing energy into the stream under the house.

And as flowing ..., now what is happening, as flowing ...?

Appliances can stay fixed and not broken.

Move to the next generation towards the present. and now what can happen?

You need to find a husband.

And as 'you need ...', now what is happening, as 'you need ...'?

233

Resistance.

Move to the next generation towards the present. and now what can happen?

I can get a job instead of a husband. and feel less pressured.

And as [that is happening], now what is happening, as [that is happening]?

I can spend some money on things I need.

Move to the next generation towards the present. and now what can happen?

I can live my own life and be happy. Don't need a man, they're trouble.

And as [that is happening], now what is happening, as [that is happening]?

I need a balance.

Move to your position. and now what can happen?

I can look on the guardian website for a new husband. I can get a job. I can sell the house. I can stop worrying. I can stop holding all the responsibility. I can have a holiday. And I can be happy.

And as [that is happening], now what is happening, as [that is happening]?

Shoulders dropping. That life's complex like a octagon with different faces being mirrored out, and depends which face I look on, and its like being stuck on one face on that and not looking at the big picture. Yup. So I can step outside that, and choose a difference face. Yep.

[END OF TRANSCRIPT]

This is a transcript showing only the female-line of the client. The male line can be explored in just the same way, or they can be explored together, generation-by-generation. As a rule one rarely needs to go across genders; the DNA's code follows male and female, so likely only the cross-grandparents have an influence, through the cultural-analogue form.

We can add past lives and their pattern of post-its in space. We can even go beyond the first life to find soul-parents, as it were, and then follow their ancestry. We can also go into cultural pronouns and the causes amongst the Gods that led to ancestral conditions.

11.3 Outside the Matrix

"Death is only the beginning." Imhotep in "The Mummy"

What happens when a person crosses the cosmological boundary into one-to-one scale? Contrary to the fears of the ego of the self beforehand, nothing untoward happens, at all. Clarity, peace, love, joy, greater awareness and sensitivity emerge naturally; nothing negative at all, as such. However, the clarity of insight into the goings on in the world around can be shocking, and the humour of the cosmic joke can be essential in dealing with the tragic comedy of human existence.

As the present self touches the old self, the selves migrate to fill more of the body. Nothing is lost, only things are gained. During the growing-up period - the frozen self now grows up to the present age in a matter of minutes, hours or days - there might be some readjustments and some temporary loss of efficiency, but this is only temporary unless (and there is an unless) a person is frozen in the growing-up moment by a new fragmentary trauma.

This is why the work is best done on retreats, with projection-free facilitators, where the time and space is present, meaning that there are no projective traumas in this critical time.

After many cosmological boundaries have been crossed, a person reaches a critical mass where the self expands through the skin. We witness people looking at their arms and reflection in amazement, feeling for the first time in their adult life what it is like to be really alive and awake.

Further boundaries can be crossed between self and other, between the self and the ancestral, the DNA patterns down the tree of life to single-cellular forms, and to the sub-cellular forms known as viruses, prions and proteins and so on. Every time a boundary is crossed, a deeper and wider knowing, clarity and insight emerges.

The experience has been likened by many Holigral graduates to being like a Samadhi, an enlightenment with experiences of pure bliss seemingly going on for ever.

Without the presence of others with similar consciousness to share the experience, despite the connected, at-one nature of the beingness, it can feel lonely to know and experience reality so differently to most humans. This is, in part, because there are still misunderstandings and separations existing between the self and the world around, probably all ancestrally inherited through the DNA, but nonetheless present in the unconscious of the self.

By gradually working at understanding all that one meets, this happens less and less, and one can enjoy playing both inside and outside of "the matrix", as some call it. Really, the only option is to have a group of friends who support each other in living life this way.

The entire universe is in the mind. The climax of the movie "Highlander" gives an idea of the experience. One can then enable other people to join this kind of consciousness; through the processes developed. As they become one-to-one scaled they report the same experiences.

A group of people emerge whose reality is in common, who rarely project, and who can see the territory rather than a map; and they seem to share the same outlook as Tibetan Buddhist philosophy, naturally, without having studied or learned any. Ouspensky writes about exactly this kind of group when he talks of G. I. Gurdjieff's "Fourth Way".

One-to-one Scale

The knowing that emerged from developing and working with the Holigral processes, was that what seemed to be happening was a re-measuring that resulted in an un-measuring; as if the problem simply had never existed. Done well, there might be no memory that there had even been a problem. This is a bit like recovering from a physical illness; as one gets better one forgets the pain very quickly.

One client was particularly striking in this regard. I saw them a few months after we worked together, and I was told that my work did not really do anything, so I asked "and how is your sleep, weight, focus, eating habits ...?" I found out that they now had no apnoea, were sleeping well, had lost five stone, were not eating snacks or drinking coffee, and had plenty of energy, and business was growing. This was typical! So, we were dealing with the processes of measurement and re-measurement.

One particular thing to mention is that attractors are overlaid, one on the other. If the earliest signals are not recognised then the later attractors will be addressed, leaving the deepest structure still intact. Either repeated iterations are needed, or most often, the womb and birth have to be visited. So I combine using the Ark Angle with other processes, such as the Re-Scaling, to address the womb traumas, to accelerate attaining permanent results.

Time

So, if we do live in a complex universe, what kind of one do we live in? I propose that we live in a six-dimensional Minkowski Space; this is a universe comprising three complex[76] space dimensions and three complex time dimensions, with past, present and future each different, complex time dimensions. And, I suggest a holding complex dimension, exterior to the six-dimensional universe (seven complex dimensions).

The normal representation of Minkowski Space is a single complex time dimension that has linear past-present-future. This, I suggest, is the effect (experience) space that is the consequence of motion on a manifold[77] in three complex time dimensions.

Plotting T-1 versus T versus T+1 (or past versus present versus future, also called delay-space) is what is used to reveal the chaotic attractors of time series – sometimes a manifold, sometimes a pattern is revealed. People have such structures in their mind-field, and these structures accurately predict apparently unpredictable human behaviour. Change the structure and you change the behaviour.

One of the strange things of having such a structure is that it allows for time to go backwards or forwards or indeed both. And, most quantum mechanical theories have terms that include backwards-in-time components that many (most?) physicists tend to prefer to ignore.

---

[76] "Complex" here equates to "real and imaginary"

[77] A manifold is a surface in delay space which defines the trajectory of movement through time.

I suggest that our experience of forward moving time may be balanced by an aspect of self, that we cannot experience, that moves backwards in time. [Although Deepak Chopra talks about "the Wizard" deep inside a person that does indeed only travel backwards in time in "The Way of the Wizard" and "Merlin".]

How do you notice a "time-going-backwards" phenomenon? Before significant events most people experience pre-shocks, just like earthquakes have pre-shocks before the "big one". Your experience is one of linear-time - "well of course this happens first" - but another way of looking at it is to consider pre-shocks to be the time "sidelobes[78]" of a big event. If you think of the emotional charge you experience before something like getting married or sitting an exam, it resembles (to a smaller degree) the actual event itself.

Where I feel some physicists have gone wrong (and I am a physicist so I can speak with some authority here) is with their concept of time, where they consider at most one complex dimension of time. Instead, in my formulation, time has three complex dimensions; past, present and future.

The present is normally the toughest dimension to understand, because one is used to thinking spatially and in relationships, but the present is a momentum dimension, and therefore not amenable to the same relating. It allows for an infinity of parallel "nows" at every point in the space dimensions and in the past-future time dimensions. It has no beginning and no end because a flow-momentum has no location in space or time.

Where are all the anti-particles? Travelling backwards in time, mostly; the few that travel forwards have equivalent particles that go backwards in time - a scary thought, and reason to avoid experiments with anti-matter. Where is all the dark matter? In the imaginary; change the assumptions and imaginary mass will be found.

---

[78] A sidelobe is a part of a wave-packet separated in time or space from the main signal. For example, a scanning radar has a primary direction, but also sends out weaker signals in other directions, and these are called sidelobes.

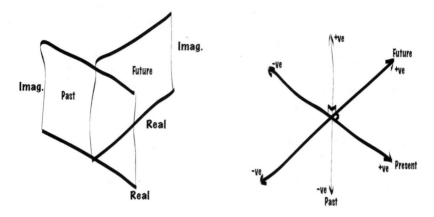

Perspectives of time being more than one complex dimension

In Chaos Theory, the "space" created by visualising a 3D display of past-versus-present-versus-future is called "delay-space embedding", and it is used to reveal the attractors in chaotic time-series. With this perspective one can see the attractors underlying behaviours, stock markets and even long-term historical evolutions. I had first used this to recognise attractors in time series for signals analysis, and so it made complete sense to me to map human patterns onto the same axes.

With this perspective, one sees that the light-image of the world around which is received at the eyes is converted into a delay-space within the brain. This makes time-varying standing waves that reflect the world around for the mind-self to perceive, thus giving the experience of "sight".

This 3D complex time also allows for Feynman's speculation that there is only one particle[79], and thus to explain entanglement and the interactions. It also allows us to understand why we experience so much matter and so little anti-matter. In my opinion, the one kind goes forward in time and the other backward, with just a little bit of each going "the wrong way".

It also allows us to understand a different nature to creation and "the big bang", instead having creation always existing in the "now", and even the

---

[79] Feynmann, as described in the book, "Genius", a biography of his life, once tried to postulate a theory that there is only one particle, and that somehow it travelled though time, repetitively, thus explaining entanglement as a self-interaction.

past being radiated out through the imaginary past, and then back through the complex space-time, into real time to the present.

It also allows us to have a different sense of "past cosmologies", including the so-called ancient black holes that existed "before time"[80]. This construct allows for time and the past or beginning of time to change depending upon the frame of reference.

Only a conscious perception from outside of "the 'matrix' of linear time" is likely to see such changes, as perceptions inside will take on board these updates as if "it has always been this way". This is like the light photon which, travelling at the speed of light, appears not to travel in time. However, to outside perspectives, which are called "frames of reference", it does indeed travel through time[81].

One possible, although highly unlikely, example of such a change of the past might be that the world was flat before the time of Galileo[82]. He required the world to orbit the sun, and so the universe complied, and we now have a universe where the earth is progressively less at the centre of the universe. Since and therefore, forever, the world has always been round.

Actually, the ancients knew the Earth was curved. It is never provable, and requires too great a conceivable magic for the modern mind. While I am not claiming this was true, I am just making a point about what is imaginable, given a structure of three dimensions of complex time.

This also also allows for a plausible science of creationism; both are possible from the frame of time now proposed. While I am all for there being a creator, it is not aligned with my beliefs to teach a distorted, Christian creator perspective. As Buddha said, "question and challenge my words".

---

[80] See the "New Scientist" magazine or similar publications for news reports on this kind of thing.

[81] Read up on Einstein's thought experiments on relativity and travelling on a light wave.

[82] Galileo Galilei, 1564-1642

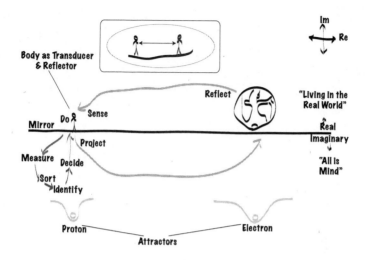

The self-other experience, and projecting cycle

The trouble with putting Humpty-Dumpty back together again is that first the pieces need assembling, and only then can a gradual sense of the whole of Humpty be seen. In hindsight, and probably after a few re-reads, I hope that understanding may dawn.

A trauma, as measurement, is not always a life-changing accident. It can be as little as a new nick-name, a school grade, positive events like marriage ceremonies, and crying in the cradle while mother is in the shower.

11.4 Conclusion of the Beyond

Blame stops nowhere but goes full circle back to oneself, completing the cosmic joke.

12 Summary

Thanks for reading this. I'm sure you will have questions if you've made it this far. Just ask them; they will be answered if they arrive by email. Try "any name you like"@holigral.com for emailing questions.

Newton's Laws, and in fact most of physics, came from his and other scientists' prior knowledge of esoterica. He was a masonic initiate, aware of the Hermetic Laws, and especially the "law of correspondence" which underlies his three laws of physics. Therefore, these laws have always applied to people, even if the scientific world had to exclude people as part of the deal with the church at the time.

By re-applying physics to people, all I am really doing is completing a circle. It fits because everything of physics was created by human minds, and therefore is a reflection of the human physicists' minds.

All I have done is to complete this circle of bringing the Physics back to explain the mind, emotions and how the spirit world interacts with ours, all with the purpose of healing and enhancing performance and quality of life for all. In terms of really understanding the contents, nothing replaces the direct experience of releasing structures and discovering the same knowing for yourself. If you have read this far, then why not take the next step and attend a retreat to ensure you live the rest of your life with a light heart, free of cares and stresses, and ready for Ma'At?

- A person is a collective of aspects, created during defining moments and epochs.

- This personal collective can be unmeasured to emerge a single self, at peace within, and at peace with the world.

- The complete human being will flow with the "right-brain" and use cognitive abilities with the "left-brain", combining both effortlessly.

- When all the aspects of self have been unmeasured, using psycho-activity, then the world around, in its entirety, becomes semipermanently psycho-active - in other words 'magical' - and signs, omens and portents again have meaning. The Grail is found and known.

◯ The processes that work to create inner peace also create group peace, and teams that can flow harmoniously at will.

◯ World peace can happen, within 16 years, if each peaceful person helps four other people per year into peace.

If we were recreating the world now, what different choices would we make? Probably none – the decisions were perfect in the moment. The resources we now have are those precisely required to solve today's problems for the benefit of tomorrow's future.

So, how would we recreate our world if we had the tools to redesign our matrices and our global matrix? Is humanity a plague, or is humanity preparing for a new stage of existence, or will nature balance the exponential growth in a dominant species that seems to be out of control? Should we care? In a few millennia the planet will self-correct. Philosophically, therefore, what is possible now?

My personal insight is that human souls can now develop more rapidly and permanently into elevated consciousness because of changes at a planetary and solar level. We inhabit a living planet, yet most occidental humans are barely conscious of their own body, let alone the magical life force flowing through other people, every single animal, plant, mineral and the spirits of the "other side".

The veils between the worlds are thinning, and this allows a new life – an expression involving the conscious experience of the whole whilst functioning in the real world.

It is possible to gain and sustain enlightenment in a very real, embodied sense, while living in "the real world". This is the purpose of the book, the trainings and the courses: to create other facilitators of this wonderful creation.

The method can be applied to ANY aspect of human endeavour and guarantee at least as efficient a solution as any other approach; because it is a universal model of reality, able to transcend and include all other modalities addressing the psyche. Among other things, the method can offer permanent solutions to:

- medium and high-functioning autism
- nonlexia and other "learning difficulties"
- depression, possession, bipolar and oversensitiveness
- addictions, compulsions and obsessions
- some major psychopathies currently considered untreatable
- dissociation and certain psycho-pathologies
- coaching, counselling and psychotherapy
- performance coaching and human development
- business resurrection, new business creation, team working in "group mind"
- world peace, and an end to war
- the "One God" problem

The method has been tested across many languages, cultures, religions and in many countries, for example, people from the following countries have attended Holigral events: UK, France, Belgium, Germany, Switzerland, Lithuania, Italy, Portugal, Spain, Hungary, Romania, Pakistan, India, Mexico, Colombia, Argentina, USA, Canada, Australia, New Zealand, Ghana, South Africa, Holland, Greece, Abu Dhabi and Japan. It works, it allows me to explain and diagnose any human phenomenon, and even some cosmological ones, and it offers us the tools to build Isaac Asimov's "Psychohistory".

A sister book, "The Spiritual Closet", addresses the more esoteric knowledge and discoveries. Why not take the risk of reading it to see the complete picture?

As it is, enjoy your dream; it's what you are here to do. If you really want to escape the dream; fine, then spend a few years at the right monastery, or a week with Holigral, and ask for "the red pill".

Pondered he did, she thought,
How and why, cause he did,
No Mind, then Peace.

- END -

13 References and Sources

The journey to creating the method involved long periods of time studying, experimenting and playing with Neuro-Linguistic Programming, Clean Language and Integral Philosophy. I collaborated with David Grove for 18 months in 2005-6, where the foundations were established.

Please consult wikipedia or other such online resources for more information on the scientific aspects like Chaos Theory and Complex Numbers.

This has been an intentionally brief resumé of the models underpinning the Holigral Method. Presently, the information on facilitating and the processes are kept for graduates, and are not disseminated more widely. It is not in the interests of clients or delegates to know them in advance, due to the mechanisms of auto-immunity that people develop to human development processes; cheating is endemic.

I had once called this work "A Natural Philosophy for Life", but unfortunately there are conflicting names in use in associated fields, not least the abbreviation being "NPL".

Under no circumstances can anyone assume permission to use any Holigral methods without the due training completed to my satisfaction and without commercial exploitation agreements having been put into place. The methods are powerful and therefore dangerous in untrained hands, and probably more so in partially-trained hands. Ultimately, it is the osmosis of the beingness that creates the results more than the processes themselves.

Recommended Reading

The following books are recommended reading for someone who wants to gain more clues as to the nature of the universe:

"Collected Works", O.M. Aivanhov - magic and insight

"Complete Andersen's Fairy Tales", H.C. Andersen - signals intelligence

"The Foundation Series", "The Robot Novels", I. Asimov - Gaia, mentalics and The Tibetan Plan

"Esoteric Philosophy" A. Bailey - plenty of cosmic jokes

"The Structure of Magic", R. Bandler, "J. Grinder" - NLP origin

"Games People Play", and other titles, E. Berne, - signals intelligence

"Attachment and Loss", J. Bowlby - essential insights

"Dictionary of Etymology", Chambers - understanding the meaning of words

"Collected Works", D. Chopra - for fun

"Jonathan Strange and Mr Norrell", S. Clarke - real magic

"Shogun", J. Clavell - understanding the Japanese

"Magician", R. Feist

"Lectures in Physics", R. Feynmann - Physics made simple

"Collected Works", S. Freud - projection

"The Path of Least Resistance - for Managers", R. Fritz - Physics in Business

"The Prophet", K. Gibran - beyond the matrix

"The Twelves Caesars", translated by M. Grant - archetypes

"Complete Grimm's Fairy Tales", brothers Grimm.

"Collected Works", G.I. Gurdjieff - about the matrix

"God's Englishman - Oliver Cromwell and the English Revolution", C. Hill

"The Iliad", Homer - the last acts of the Gods

"Warfare in the Ancient World", R. Humble - "The Great King" model

"Celtic Fairy Tales", J. Jacobs

"The Wheel of Time series", R. Jordan - magic

"Collected Works", C.G. Jung - group unconscious, archetypes, alchemy

"The Dune Series", F. Herbert - understanding possession and folding space

"The Urban Shaman", S.K. King - modern, practical magic.

"Well-loved Tales", The Ladybird Collection

"New Larousse Encyclopedia of Mythology" - understanding the Gods

"Metaphors in Mind", J. Lawley & P. Tompkins - an introduction to "Clean Language"

"Linear Algebra", S. Lipschutz - for Hermitian Matrices

"The Nicholas Linnear Novels", E.V. Lustbader - understanding Japanese magic

"The Galactic Milieu Saga", J. May - cultivating psychic powers

"Elric of Melbone & Dorian Hawkmoon novels", M. Moorcock - Archetypes

"Watchmen", A. Moore, D. Gibbons - the superhero evolution

"The Bible", Moses et.al. - the story that created all the problem

"The Story of Decipherment", M. Pope - how not to understand hieroglyphs

"His Dark Materials", P. Pullman - parallel universes, animal guides, persona flex

"Physics for the Enquiring Mind", Rogers - an introduction to thinking Physics

"Roget's Thesaurus" - for the structure of the English language

"The Harry Potter Novels", J.K. Rowling - for hints as to magic

"Various Poems", Rumi - beyond the matrix

"The Fifth Discipline" P. Senge - an introduction to systems thinking

"The Collected Works", W. Shakespeare - the archetypal stories of mankind

"Los Mayos", N.G. Solano - clues as to Mayan script

"A History of the English-Speaking Peoples", W. Spencer-Churchill

"Business Dynamics: Systems Thinking and Modeling for a Complex World", John D. Sterman - systems thinking applied, large-scale.

"The Bartimaeus Trilogy", J. Stroud - entities

"The Prose Edda", S. Sturluson - easy-to-visualise languaging

"The History of Middle Earth", J.R.R. Tolkien - for an alternate cosmology

"Collected Works", E. Tolle - for another perspective on "nowing"

"The Kybalion", (The Three Initiates, featuring Hermes Trismegistus)

"Collected Works", K. Wilber - an introduction to Integral Theories

"In Search of the Trojan War", M. Wood - piecing together the history post-Moses

"The Secret of Crete", R. Wunderlich - an alternative view on the purpose of Knossos

"The Great Book of Amber", R. Zelazney - chaos and structure

Recommended Watching - Filmography

All films are likely refuges for dissociated aspects, and the modern films represent the evolving edge of the group mind, they are a reflection. The following films might help understanding what is going on.

Excalibur - the secrets of the Grail

Hot Fuzz - signals

Kenny - authenticity

Credits - Alphabetical

Blossie Mountjoy, for mentoring and being.

Charles Wansbrough for funding the initial Ark Angle development, and his insight into the energy movements as the work happens.

Charlie Dancey for designing and building the Ark Angle.

David Grove, for many reasons, for being an equal in innovating the work, a comrade and friend.

Dr Jenny Leonard, for her psychological evaluation of The Holigral Method.

Josie Saunders, for her continued support; none of this would be, without her.

Julie Sellars for our collaboration in autism and learning difficulties.

Nicholas Drew for the cover illustration.

Sarah Kent for being involved in the discussions and guinea-pigging of many new processes.

Stuart Blan for being a fellow Physicist, sportsman and madman.

Tania Korsak for our collaboration cross-pollenating her anthropological developmental model and the Holigral Method.